NATURAL LAW
AND THE ETHICS OF LOVE

NATURAL LAW
AND
THE ETHICS OF LOVE

A New Synthesis

by WILLIAM A. SPURRIER

THE WESTMINSTER PRESS
Philadelphia

Book Design by Dorothy Alden Smith

Published by The Westminster Press ®
Philadelphia, Pennsylvania

PRINTED IN THE UNITED STATES OF AMERICA

Library of Congress Cataloging in Publication Data

Spurrier, William Atwell.
  Natural law and the ethics of love: a new synthesis.

  Bibliography: p.
  1. Christian ethics.   2. Natural law.   3. Social
ethics.   I. Title.
BJ1251.S69   177'.6   74–6211
ISBN 0–664–20702–2

To Victor L. Butterfield,
    president of Wesleyan University 1943–1967,
    whose passion for rational values in education
    inspired many of us to seek deeper levels
    of meaning and more practical applications
    of both knowledge and values.

Contents

INTRODUCTION

The need for both love and law today would seem to be very great. The usual public view of politics as dirty and immoral is underlined by the disclosures of Watergate. It is said in defense that "dirty tricks" have long been practiced by both parties anyhow, and this statement is widely believed. In addition, economic favoritism by those in political power and the wide gap between rich and poor do not support the idea that public morals command much respect.

Meanwhile, in the area of personal behavior, many young people accuse older people of hypocrisy in their cries for "law and order." And many of those over thirty charge those under thirty with moral anarchy, loose love, and looser sex. "Do your own thing" seems to be the slogan for no rules and no ethics.

On one level, then, one could make out a pretty convincing case that contemporary life, both public and private, is indeed quite immoral. On the other hand, most persons do not believe that *they* are particularly immoral. The natural human response is to blame others: it is always some other group that is mostly evil. One of Senator George McGovern's 1972 campaign mistakes was his failure to understand this point. He made many calls for the nation to return to righteousness. But he failed to understand that most of us believed that *we* had not departed from it. So who needed to return? In the opinion of many hard-hats, middle Americans, Establishment people, and those of us over thirty, it was the longhairs, radicals, and McGovernites who needed to return to righteousness. Yet they, on the other hand, could rightly accuse both Democratic and Republican administrations and the Establishment for lying to the public about many things, among them events in Vietnam and Cambodia, as well as illegal campaign contributions and other cover-ups. Thus, the mote in the other's eye always seems greater than the beam in one's own.

On a deeper level, however, there does seem to be a common concern for a better way of life, for higher levels of justice, for more integrity, and if possible, for a more effective morality or ethics. Some may yearn for the old-fashioned virtues, others for a new, nuclear-age morality, and most of us just grope for ethical guidance. What is common to all of us, perhaps, is the deep hunger for some kind of love and some kind of law that will offer us both guidance and the possibility of a higher quality of living.

This small book attempts to offer at least a start. The Introduction discusses briefly the present status of Christian ethics and whether such ethics are still viable. The remainder of the book presents a model as well as a way in which these ethics might be used more effectively. It suggests that an alliance be made between two of the main traditions in Christianity (Roman Catholic natural law ethics and Protestant situational love ethics), and finally it indicates a new and better way of practicing Christian ethics.

Our first concern is with the problem of whether Christian ethics are possible today both within the household of Christianity and in the world outside the church.

Internally, many critics would argue that there is no such thing as recognizable Christian ethics. There are many versions of ethics, most of them different, usually mixed up with cultural and secular mores, and some of them are even contradictory. For example, one can still find devout conservative

Christians holding rigidly to strict moral rules against drinking, dancing, and most forms of sex. By contrast, many more liberal Christians seem to regard most codes as highly "relative," but scarcely relevant. They speak of Christianity as "a way of life," freed from the tyranny of rules, and indeed (according to the title of one sermon on ethics) as "the dance of life."

Or, please note—the critics say—that the Roman Catholic Church is against birth control devices but most Protestants are in favor of them. Or look at the heavy emphasis Catholics put on natural law rules, while most "radical" Protestants emphasize the need for a person "to know the situation" before he can determine what is the right or wrong thing to do.

In other areas of church life, critics point out with equal sharpness the lack of moral guidance on the part of the churches. On the one hand, the varieties of ethics cause the church to give a variety of answers or advice, which results in confusion. Thus, one minister says that the President is the greatest peacemaker in modern times; another one says that the same President is one of the worst war-makers in recent history. On the other hand, many persons feel that the church is not so much guilty of diverse moral advice as it is of silence in the face of obvious moral evils and injustices. It does seem that the record of the churches' moral protest against racism, economic exploitation, and excessive bombing tactics in war has been dismally poor—except for a few persons here and there. To be sure, there have been papal pleas and denominational resolutions calling for peace, justice, and love. But they are couched in such abstract and vague terms as to offend no one and to point to no specific policy or alternative. Such pronouncements sound like answers to some Gallup poll question such as: If there were no Communists or other evils around, would you be in favor of peace or war?

Thus, within the household of faith one could find considerable evidence for the argument that there is no such thing as Christian ethics per se. Furthermore, even if there were, such ethics are very seldom applied. And when they are applied, they are either vague and meaningless, diverse and confused, or contradictory.

Externally, in the world outside the church, many critics would also argue that the application of Christian ethics is not possible today. Many feel that the modern world is too complex, too fast moving and powerful for Christian ethics. While such ethics may be noble and even true, they are, alas, too impractical. Life was simpler in the olden days, one might argue, and an ancient Palestinian ethic was practical then. But now, life and our problems today are vast and vicious. The world is too much with us. For instance, how could the Sermon on the Mount deal with awesome nuclear problems, gigantic economic conglomerates, or brutal crime in the streets?

Thus, faced with internal weakness and external complexity, one can make an impressive case for the view that Christian ethics are just no longer relevant or practical today.

The intent of this book is to show how Christian ethics can be effective today by combining the best features of the Roman Catholic ethic and the best aspects of the Protestant ethic, and by suggesting a better way of using and applying Christian ethics to contemporary problems.

Responses to the Critics' Analysis. The first appropriate response to criticism is to acknowledge its validity. Any knowledgeable person will readily admit that there is truth in the various charges briefly outlined above. Indeed, those of us on the inside of the church could list many more of our weaknesses. Precisely because we are on the inside we know much better than those on the outside how weak and ineffectual we really are. And few would disagree with the critical assessment of the violent and complex nature of the external or secular world. So let us then confess the truth of the critics' observations.

However, most thoughtful observers would also agree that such a critique is not the whole truth or the full picture. Even if such were the whole situation now, it does not mean that the plight of Christian ethics will always remain what it is at present. Thus, the obvious point has to be made that the misuse or corruption of a thing does not necessarily mean that the thing itself is evil or useless. People use and misuse cars, money, religion, sex, love, and friendship but clearly do not abandon these because they are misused. It *is* essential to note well the weaknesses and misuses of Christian ethics and take into account most seriously the valid judgments of our critics.

The second response, however, is to fill out the larger picture by pointing out the nature of the things that have been corrupted or perhaps ignored. This is to say that there are resources of experience, wisdom, and insight within the two main Christian traditions of Catholicism and Protestantism. For example, most people seemed to agree that the just war theory with its seven criteria for determining the justice of a particular war was pretty well outmoded, inapplicable, and therefore useless. But when the agony of the Vietnam war grew and people groped for guidance, pro or con, the seven criteria proved to be most realistic and helpful.

In addition, within Protestantism there has been a growing restlessness among many about the lack of standards for moral behavior. While the high emphasis on love and responsible individualism is exhilarating and attractive, serious and sensitive persons would like to know how one determines what is responsible, and by what criteria or guidelines one evaluates his "situation." Meanwhile, in Catholicism, particularly Roman Catholicism, many persons are restless and feel constricted by too many rules too narrowly interpreted. They are rereading the Bible and the Reformers, and thereby getting a glimpse of the power of the Spirit and the spontaneity of love. Thus, it would seem that Protestants need "laws" and Catholics need "love." As a result, each is finding resources in the other's tradition that might be most helpful.

Similarly, many Christians are banding together to find new ways of applying Christian ethics. There is a healthy ferment within the traditions. Scholars are reexamining everything; the laity are most willing to challenge the priesthood and the institution; some clergy are pioneering in new forms of social action, new ways of doing Christian ethics, and new types of liturgy for worship. Thus, our own weak situation and the truth of the critiques invite us to reexamine and recover the original resources within our traditions and then relate them to new secular resources that also appear. This process is exemplified by the increasing cooperation between ministers and psychiatrists, ethicists and social scientists, pastors and medical doctors.

It is not enough to assert that there are powerful and practical resources within Christian ethics and within the traditions. We must also be more specific and show what they are, describe them, define them, and see how they may help us to be more effective in our ethical and moral life. Thus, the first part of this book attempts to describe Christian ethics as found in the two main traditions of Catholicism and Protestantism. Next, we shall try to evaluate critically both ethical processes in order to sort out the strengths and weaknesses of each emphasis. It is in this section where we try more completely to respond to the critics' analysis. It is here that we, too, are critics, and like all responsible evaluators, we intend not just to say what is wrong, but to sift out what is true, essential, and authentic.

Another response to the critic—as most informed people know—is that when one engages in a critique of ethics and values, before long one is forced back to theological values and assumptions. For example, when one tries to establish a priority of values, one is immediately dependent upon some prior criterion of what is most worthwhile. Even when a methodology is chosen, its selection is determined by one's theology as, for instance, in the classical argument between deductive and inductive thinking. In the field of ethics this means that one may believe that a system of laws and principles can be understood, brought to a problem, and then deductively applied to the issues. By contrast, the opponents will argue that one must first find out what the issues and complexities are in the given situation, and then and only then can he inductively arrive at some moral guideline. The point to note is that this conflict over the best method is not a tactical argument, it is a basic philosophical or theological problem.

Similarly, the importance of a theological approach is further underlined when one considers how ethics are to be used. For example, if a person's doctrine of man is one that sees human nature as essentially good, and if evil is to be explained largely by ignorance, then it is likely that such a person will believe that noble ideals and education will be the salvation of man. Or, by contrast, if one's theology sees man as essentially evil and utterly dependent upon God's grace, then that person's ethics will probably be personally pious, socially conservative, and generally passive.

These and other illustrations show why there is a necessary and inevitable relation between theology and ethics. Thus, presumptuous and precarious as it may appear, another section of this book will be devoted to a critical theological analysis of what kinds of theology will lead toward the most effective kind of Christian ethics.

The first half of this book, then, is an attempt to sort out what seem to me to be the essential ethical ingredients in the two great traditions, to find those theological insights and doctrines which would enable us to use the ethics most effectively, and then to suggest how the best of Catholicism and Protestantism could be allied, or synthesized, in order that we might draw deeply on their respective treasures while avoiding the weaknesses of each.

The last half of the book is the real test. It is relatively easy to say that Catholic natural law is this and the Protestant ethic is that. It is still fairly easy to suggest that such and such a doctrine of man or theory of historical understanding is better than some other view. But clearly the real test of both theology and ethics is whether they are relevant and practical, whether they can make a significant difference in contemporary life.

Therefore we have deliberately chosen two of the most complex and difficult moral problems we can think of—one in the area of social ethics and one in the area of personal ethics. The two awesome issues are: (1) nuclear war and present international balance-of-power politics and (2) sex. It is our conviction that if we can show how Christian ethics can deal significantly with giant international problems, then it should be fairly clear how we may also deal with other social issues such as domestic politics and economics. Similarly, if we can show how Christian ethics can offer helpful guidance in the explosive area of sex, then we ought to be able to find further practical help in the less volatile areas of life.

A cursory glance at the size of this volume will indicate some of its limits. Obviously this book does not cover all the major problems of ethics. We do not claim to offer here a guide through every obstacle in life. Rather, the purpose is to describe a theological-ethical model of Christian ethics. It is a plan that we believe can be used effectively and relevantly. The last sections of the book contain other suggestions on how the model can be used.

What is important, therefore, is not every detail or specific comment. If critics can see better ways of improving or using the model, then we shall be grateful to have provided even a springboard to something better.

It should be equally obvious that not all Christians will agree with everything in this book. Indeed, some may even reject in toto the model and/or the way it is applied. Given the cultural history of diversity and the natural limitations of this author, no universal agreement is expected. On the other hand, I am convinced that a large number of Catholics and Protestants will find substantial agreement here, and that there can be enough critical alliance to produce significant and effective ethical action.

PERSONAL PREFACE

Hardly an ethicist is now alive who hasn't seen the need for some kind of Christian ethical process that would include the best features of Roman Catholic natural law and of the Protestant situational love approach. Of course, there are some in each camp who see only the evils in the other system and who, therefore, are relatively content with what they have. And there are a few iconoclasts who want no system at all. These are matched by the even fewer souls who think that divine law has been accurately captured by Thomas Aquinas or themselves. But surely the majority of professional ethicists now see the desirability for some kind of alliance or synthesis of the two traditions.

On the positive side, I enjoy the freedom and flexibility of the situational love ethic. It reinforces all my antinomian feelings, justifies my distaste for legalistic nitpicking and rubric throwing. Barth's and Bultmann's affirmations of what it means to be free from cultural mores by being "in Christ" stir my soul. The high emphasis on love as opposed to tradition, laws, rules, and codes frees the spirit and makes one feel religious in the best sense of the word.

At the same time, I am equally impressed with the rational integrity and precision with which a natural law ethic can discern and define moral goods and evils. There is a lot of thoughtless talk and careless action going on in the name of justice or love or some other high ideal. It is good to have a sharp tool that can dissect sense from nonsense, that can see various levels of justice or violence and define them realistically and clearly.

On the negative side, I am appalled at the individual anarchy and the evils committed in the name of love under the aegis of "contextual realism" and "a crisis situation." Often in my own moral decisions I am not really sure how I get "from here to there." Am I really translating God's love through me to a political action? Or is my decision to take that action infected by some of my egoism, my desires, and my cultural biases? Am I really loving in a Christian way?

Similarly with the natural law ethic; we are all familiar with its many historical misuses: the narrow rigidities, the overly strict application of minute rules to the neglect of human concern, and—on the broader front—the imperious claim to know God's will on specifics such as abortion, or the unqualified assurance that the church can clearly know divine law.

These experiences, among others, lead me to yearn for an "impossible dream." Can an ethical synthesis be effected between Roman Catholic natural law and the Protestant situational love ethic, an alliance that retains the virtues of each and avoids the vices of both?

Much of the groundwork for this synthesis has been done or is being done. The need has been established as seen in the works of the "middle axiom" school of John C. Bennett (formerly of Union Theological Seminary) and J. H. Oldham (formerly of Cambridge University), in the writings of Paul Ramsey (especially his *Deeds and Rules in Christian Ethics*), and in at least two writers in the natural law tradition, namely, Kenneth E. Kirk and Herbert Waddams.

The most important theological groundwork is found in James M. Gustafson's *Christ and the Moral Life*, James E. Sellers' *Theological Ethics*, and, in the natural law tradition, Josef Fuchs' *Natural Law*.[1]

These and other works are indicative of the significance of the problems at hand, of the need for the theological basis of the synthesis, and of the trends or probable future directions. This book will attempt to outline an example of the model of the synthesis and to suggest how such a synthesis could be made to work more effectively and realistically than present approaches in some of our contemporary moral dilemmas.

Meanwhile, here are a few brief guides that may help to clarify the author's use of certain basic concepts and terms.

Love and Law, Geneva and Rome. "Geneva" and "Rome" are not to be taken literally, geographically, or historically. They are used only as shorthand symbols. Most persons are familiar with "Rome" as the symbolic word for Roman Catholicism, and no one infers that thereby the discussion of Catholicism is limited to that city. Likewise, "Geneva" is only a single word to encompass a sprawling Protestantism.

Similarly, in equating "law" with Rome, we do not mean to imply that Catholicism knows nothing of love, or that natural law is absent from Protestantism. So—oversimplified and symbolical—our shorthand formula is this: "Rome" designates Roman Catholicism's natural law ethics; "Geneva" designates Protestantism's situational love ethics. We are aware that Calvin would indeed be surprised to find "Geneva" so used as a symbol. We are also aware that there are many groups of Christians who could not be fitted under any special label no matter how symbolic or broadly interpreted.

In spite of the perils of labeling, and within a broad understanding of the symbols, I believe there is such a thing as *the* Christian faith, and that a sizable number of persons want to stand under the banner of that faith even though they do not agree on everything or claim to have the answers to all problems. After all, one authentic New Testament affirmation was, "I believe; help my unbelief!" (Mark 9:24.)

Pietism. This is a sizable theological-ethical position which is present in all denominations and Christian traditions. It asserts that *the* function of religion is one's personal relationship to God. It insists that the gospel of salvation by Jesus Christ has and should have no relation to politics, economics, or other social issues. For example, looking back on his career as an evangelist, the Rev. Billy Graham recently said in an interview (as reported by Jack Thomas of *The Boston Globe*, Jan. 8, 1974): "I'm going to stay further away from partisan politics than I've ever stayed before. . . . I've learned how complicated things can be. . . . I think that my ministry is going to be more moral and spiritual and less political." Thus, pietistic ethics is almost entirely personal and is often specifically against any social ethics.

Moral Theology. This is the study which tries to relate certain theological doctrines to moral decisions and actions. Thus, for example, the doctrine of the nature of man is of crucial importance in figuring out one's moral response either to evil within one's self or to an evil action done to one's person. If one believes that man is basically good and does little evil, although a few "mistakes" do occur, his response to the "evildoer" may be rational, idealistic, and persuasive. On the other extreme, if one's doctrine of man sees man as virtually psychopathically evil, he will probably "shoot first and talk afterward." So moral theology tries to work out rational and clear relationships between thelogy and moral responses.

Ethics. In this book I use the word "ethics" to connote almost entirely general principles such as justice, freedom, equality, brotherhood, honesty, integrity, and the like.

Morals. This word largely refers to specific choices, actions, and deeds. One decides to give fifty dollars to the United Fund; one votes for a particular tax or civil rights bill; one tells a "white lie" to an aging friend. These are specific deeds —moral actions—and they may represent the application of general ethical principles. "Thou shalt tell the truth" is an ethical principle. But when my attention is drawn to an unbecoming hat on the head of a lady friend, what is the specific moral choice? Shall I tell her "the ugly truth" and hurt her feelings or tell her a semineutral "white lie" and save the friendship? The highest standard of love may determine the specific moral choice: a white lie. Yet the negative principle of no lying is also relevant here in the analysis. It makes us aware of the compromise and the ethical mixture of truth and falsehood. In sum, however, ethics are concerned with general principles, while morals deal with specific actions.

Natural Law. This term does not refer to the laws used in science, such as the laws of gravity or thermodynamics, or chemical formulas. In the field of theology and ethics, natural law really means almost literally "rational law." This theory is derived from the belief that there are rational structures embedded in the process of life; there are realities "out there" in the natural structure of life that can be observed or discovered by man's rational mind. A rational structure in nature is seen by man's reason. An example of such a reality would be the principle of social order, i.e., the need for some kind of minimal state or government. The particular type of state may vary, but the need for a state is a natural-rational condition. Similarly, "Thou shalt not murder within the tribe" is a natural-rational, universal principle. This is not an artificial rule "devised by priests to keep the masses down"; it is a rather obvious "natural" principle that helps provide natural survival or protection. Natural law, then, refers to general ethical principles that can be rationally derived from natural structures in life.

Situational Love Ethics. Although the word "situational" is relatively new, this type of ethics is very ancient. Old or new, the term refers to an emphasis placed upon the nature of the moral choice, rather than the application of principles or rules. Augustine, for example, once said, "Love God and do as you please." His emphasis here indicates the primacy for him of Christian love and his distaste for too many rigid rules or meticulously applied principles. Similarly, today's "situationalist," impatient with codes and rules, stresses Christian love, but also insists on searching out the ingredients in the problem at hand. He wants to find out as much as he can about the situation—what is involved, what the alternatives might be, what is good or bad, and what is practical. One applies love to the situation—hence, situational love ethics.

After teaching ethics for over twenty-five years, the author could not begin to list individually and fairly all the persons to whom he is indebted. It is obvious that many students contributed much to whatever growth and wisdom I have attained. But so, too, have many friends and colleagues; so, too, has the church—often in negative ways. I get so angry and frustrated at its picayune concerns and fearful timidity that I have been forced to ask: Well, what should we be doing? So out of negative reaction have often come positive results. Overall, however, I believe my chief acknowledgment of gratitude is owed to Wesleyan University. For this is where it all happened. The freedom, not just permitted, but encouraged, has been exhilarating. The growth of the Department of Religion from two to ten colleagues has been most stimulating and reinforcing. The history of interdisciplinary study, a passionate concern of one of the university's great presidents, Victor L. Butterfield, has been a subtle but pervasive and enriching influence. So on the general level, I wish to acknowledge my academic home—Wesleyan University. On the specific level, I am most grateful to Ms. Trudy Marth for her clever deciphering of my handwritten hieroglyphics and her arduous task in typing the manuscript. Also many thanks are due to Mrs. Verna Spaeth, who rescued the manuscript from drowning in a sea of syntactical and grammatical deficiencies. Finally, of course, I owe much to my wife for cheerfully putting up with my vacant stares and preoccupied mind while I was doing the writing.

W. A. S.

Wesleyan University
Middletown, Connecticut

Chapter
I

ROMAN CATHOLIC NATURAL LAW ETHICS

It is essential, I think, to offer a critical analysis of natural law ethics in order to show which features are desirable and which are to be avoided. This is inevitably and necessarily a personal evaluation. Others might want to retain this and drop that, or vice versa. I would not claim that my lists are the only possible ones. Let it be said that this is just an example rather than an exhaustive treatise or an authoritative scroll.

Desirable Elements
in Natural Law Ethics

1. At its best, Rome, via Thomas Aquinas and others, has always insisted that love is the prime mover in any Christian ethical system. References to "love-bearing" reason (and faith), Augustine's conversion of the cardinal virtues into the four forms of love, and Aquinas' paraphrase of Paul to the effect that there is no true virtue without love are found in most works on moral theology. God's love as revealed in and through Christ is clearly the beginning, the norm, and the goal of all Christian ethics. This needs to be stressed because many Romans forget it, and most Protestants don't know that it stands behind natural law—at least in theory if not always in practice.

2. The rational attempt to order and define moral goods and evils is certainly a noble task. Surely our interior life and external social history are filled with disorder, chaos, and irrationality. It is essential therefore to try to find some bases of rationality and sense, at least inside of ourselves. And the fact that reason cannot solve all problems is no excuse for not using it to its fullest.

3. Similarly, when we are faced with complexity and ambiguity, reason is the best tool to use in sorting out the subtle blends of goods and evils and in discerning the moral mixtures of the options available.

4. As time goes by, the various principles, values, and ideals that are accumulated can be helpful in evaluating or illuminating moral dilemmas. This same "moral tradition" can also help us in passing on to the next generation the substance of our moral life, and it can enable the individual to understand better how he gets "from here to there." Clear and teachable principles can be useful guides to ethical decisions.

5. Finally, because natural law emphasizes reason and principles, it provides us with a system of fairly common checks and balances to the individual conscience. There is here at least a better chance for common experience, common witness, and common action to occur; the resources are available and usable insofar as they are the products of reason and common faith. In short, we are saying that there is a valid and necessary place for the church in a Christian ethical system.

Undesirable Elements in Natural Law Ethics

1. The most familiar weakness, of course, is the misuse of natural law in the form of rigid definitions and applications to specifics. The historical record of the liturgical corruptions need not be repeated, e.g., one must say X number of "Hail Mary's" for Y number of tiny sins, and earn indulgences for Z

number of days less in purgatory. More recently, the simple process of casuistry seems to make any action justifiable in the name of reason.

2. While building up a tradition of principles and practices has its virtues as noted in item 4 above, it also has its great weaknesses. In fact, "tradition" has often resulted in making certain principles or rules absolutistic. Thus, decrees about celibacy and abortion have become absolute ethical laws. Rubrics or canon law often get in the way of obvious human caring—as when Holy Communion is refused to a non-Roman Christian, or when someone is excommunicated for some ecclesiastically defined mortal sin. The emphasis in the administration of natural law is not on what is the loving thing to do, but on what is canonically legal and ecclesiastically practical.

3. There are no adequate explanations within natural law of how and why certain priorities of values or morals are established. For example, why should the life of the monastic be regarded as superior to that of the man in the world, or celibacy as greater than noncelibacy? To be sure, in formal terms, *moral* superiority is not claimed. But *some* kind of superiority is affirmed one way or another. Bernard Häring, for example, unwittingly provides such a value judgment when he describes a man who left his wife and nine children to become a hermit. Häring refers to the man's decision as "the heroic sacrifice of Brother Klaus." There is no mention of the sacrifice of the wife and children, nor is there any hint that there might have been several ingredients of egotism, hostility, escapism, and the like, in the motives of Klaus. We are clearly to infer that from pure motives Klaus sacrified for the "higher life." [2] Could one not argue that Christ could be even better or at least equally served by raising nine children to the glory of God? So, what is the basis for the inference of superiority?

4. Since it is acknowledged that reason cannot handle all problems and that diversity of honest rational opinion does

occur, Rome solves the problem by a retreat into the magisterium. (The magisterium, in Catholic usage, is the church's
teaching authority and power, part of which may be papal
infallibility.) Thus, in essential and basic cases such as those
concerned with divorce, euthanasia, and celibacy, all doubt is
dispelled and *the* answer is provided. Of course, this is a
theological issue, but its ethical effect is enormous. Therefore,
it seems to me, the issue of the magisterium must be acknowledged and accounted for. From my theological-ethical position
I have to assert that the retreat to magisterial decision, if not
to infallibility, is a weakness because it assumes a human
knowledge of the divine will on specific moral behavior. I
do not see how man—collectively or individually—can claim
such clear and unambiguous knowledge. And why is it that,
almost without exception, such divine specifics have very
close effects on either the authority of the church or the
efficacy of its administration? Some ringing semiabsolutist
statement condemning the exploitation of the poor or mas-
sacres in Vietnam and Bangladesh would have more objective
authenticity than would a statement of canonical rules on the
Eucharist.

Critical Issues

It should be fairly clear that most of the criticisms and
weaknesses we have described are due not to the natural law
ethic itself, but to human nature (sin) and theological assumptions. While we cannot deal adequately here with the
theological issues at stake, perhaps it is important to note the
central relevant problems that need common study and discussion. The critical issues are, I believe, as stated in the following paragraphs.

Epistemology. The classic debate on whether reason is
partly corrupted by sin or not must be continued perhaps in
different ways. I suspect, for example, that the issue should

not be cast in the form of pure reason vs. total depravity. A more fruitful approach might be closer to an empirical method than to a formal method. That is, after we have recognized that there are limits to reason, a more rigorous examination of what the limits are and where the causes of limits and/or "corruption" really lie might bring us closer to agreement. In any case, the need for reexamining the respective epistemologies is enormous. I would argue, for instance, that the chief reason for the Roman neglect of the primacy of love in the use of natural law is precisely due to the belief that informed human reason can discern the divine law. As a result, the major Roman effort is put into discerning, defining, and applying reason. The proof of this assertion is that in any central ethical debate by Roman Catholics within their own house, at any level, one almost never finds anyone raising the question, "Is this the loving thing to do?" or, "Have we correctly applied love here?" Instead, the arguments and the decisions are usually offered in terms such as: "This is licit," "This is canonical," "*Nihil obstat*" ("Nothing hinders") or, on the other hand, "This is a violation of natural law."

In short, there is in my judgment a too close identification of man's reason with divine reason, and the resulting effect is an attempt to use and prove that claim. The end result is too heavy an emphasis on the rational and legal aspects of ethics to the neglect of the loving, human side.

The Views of Christ. James Gustafson has done a superb job in outlining how the various views of Christ influence one's approach and use of ethics.[3] With a gentle but incisive pen he indicates how, for example, if one views Christ primarily as the "justifier," a man will emphasize his inner freedom in Christ and therefore feel quite free from external rules, customs, and cultures, if not principles. On the other hand, if one sees Christ as the "teacher," he is likely to be a moral idealist and try to follow or imitate the high ideals of love, justice, and sacrifice. Or again, if one sees Jesus as the "sanctifier," whose grace enables one to seek the *summum bonum,* then one's ethic will be filled with natural law principles, which are seen as rational guides to final good.

As Gustafson points out, it is futile to argue about which view is the correct one. The important duty before us is to see the need for the many sides of the meaning of Christ. The particularly urgent ethical need is to determine how one uses the full Christ, or how one decides which part of Christ's work is the most relevant to whatever moral problem is at hand. It is relatively easy theologically to assert the need for the fullness of the various views of Christ. The really difficult task is to apply them to ethics and moral action. I hope that in his next book Gustafson will attempt just that.

The Nature of God. One's view of the nature of God, as one's view of Christ, will also influence one's ethical system and moral behavior. For example, if with Calvin one believes in a doctrine of elective salvation, then one is likely to believe or to hope that his moral behavior will be a sign of such an election. Or if one sees the will of God in existential terms à la Bultmann, he is likely to be anti natural law and, instead, likely to emphasize personal freedom, grace, immediacy, and self-fulfillment. Here again, I very much doubt if choices must be made between various views of the nature of God. Rather, the task is to find the balance in which most views ought to be held and the emphasis that may be required at certain times. On the other hand, we do not want an easy eclecticism that clouds over significant or important differences. It may be, for example, that a rigid Calvinistic doctrine of double predestination cannot and should not be reconciled with a universal love/salvation doctrine. In such cases, the differences *and* their implications for ethics and moral action should be clearly described. For the most part, however, I believe most views of God between contemporary Romans and Protestants can be held in a creative balance, even tension. But if this is true, the work needs to be done and spelled out as clearly as possible.

Sin. Another full-dress theological review of the doctrines of sin is not necessary. But two areas need highlighting. First, mutual and charitable discussions between Romans and Protestants should occur about the comparative emphasis put on the types of sin which abound. Rome has tended to place a heavy emphasis on many small sins to the neglect of major sins such as racism, war, and economic injustice. Similarly, in the past, conservative Protestantism has railed against sex, smoking, and drinking, while remaining silent or even supporting racism, war, and injustice. A reordering of priorities in the doctrines of sin is obviously needed.

Second, a candid self-criticism and correction of actual ecclesiastical sins is required for the health of the church and the proper use of the natural law ethic. As suggested earlier, many of the weaknesses of the Roman ethic are not in the ethic itself, but in its misuse. Thus, acknowledgment of some of the sinful misuses could be the prelude to proper use.

Summary. In contributing to the proposed ethical synthesis, let the natural law ethic offer the power of rational discernment, order, and clarity of moral goods and evils; let it affirm the need and relevance of guiding the illuminating principles; and let it reassert and reemphasize Christian love as the ambience of the whole system.

Chapter II

PROTESTANT SITUATIONAL LOVE ETHICS

It is essential, I think, to offer a critical analysis of Protestant situational love ethics similar to that given Roman Catholic natural law ethics in the preceding chapter. If we are to know the ingredients necessary for a synthesis, we must know which are desirable and which are not.

Desirable Elements in Protestant Situational Love Ethics

1. The primary and weighty emphasis on Christian love is the heart of this ethical tradition, and as such it surely reflects the primary emphasis in the Gospels. For the Protestant, at least in theory (as for the Roman), God's love as revealed in and through Christ is the beginning power, the norm, and the goal of the life of the Christian. Ethically speaking, I like to state it thus: "Love is the one and only absolute and therefore all else is relative to it."

2. A secondary but also weighty emphasis is placed on the necessity of flexible application of love to concrete situations. Precisely because God's love is power, among other things, it can be expressed in a number of ways. Or the situation itself may require a number of responses. For example, at

one moment a child may need the restraint of a just love, at another moment, tender forgiveness, at still another time, a vigorous call to caring action. The Christian "lover" is especially sensitive to how love might be expressed in a crisis situation or in a complex and ambiguous problem. He does not want love to be narrowed or confined or shut out by rigid rules or "previous experience."

3. The Protestant situationalist points out the importance of the word "situation." By this he means that the nature of the problem must be more adequately understood if one is to express and apply Christian love most efficiently. After many years of countless liberal Protestant church resolutions calling for peace, brotherhood, "Vote for Honesty," etc., it became quite obvious that such intentions, while noble and ethical, were almost totally futile. In some cases, concentration on ideal goals actually deterred persons from imperfect but realizable improvements. Thus, in trying to apply love to a concrete problem, say, a more just tax structure, the situationalist asserts that one must learn more about the hard facts of economics, taxation, and whatever else is required for adequate understanding. In short, Christian love, the right motives, the noble goals are not enough; secular factual information is equally necessary if our moral action is to be effective and relevant. Samuel Johnson's famous remark is often revived: "Sir, Hell is paved with good intentions." Similarly, the situationalist reminds us that good motives are not enough; one must know what is the real "situation."

4. The fourth virtuous ingredient in this ethical tradition is its dedication to openness, to new truths, insights, and methods regardless of their source. This basic attitude helps one to be more receptive to the uncomfortable prophet, the secular radical, the cautious conservative, the Hindu seer, or whomever. By definition, for the situationalist, truth can come from any culture, religion, person, or event. Therefore, one must be open at all times to all sources and methods. At its best,

this was the true and original spirit of liberalism in Western
culture and Protestant ethics.

Undesirable Elements in Protestant
Situational Love Ethics

1. As others have noted, one of the most common weaknesses in this love ethic is that almost all its exponents fail to
define Christian love. In fact, some do not even use the label
"Christian." Thus, one is not sure what the author or the doer
means by "love." In our culture, where the word has so many
connotations, it is clearly irresponsible not to make clear what
one means by this "love" concept. Granted, the task is basically
a theological one; nevertheless, because it *is* the heart of the
ethic, it must be defined and explained. This failure by the
proponents of the situational love ethic has contributed to the
widespread misuse of the Christian love ethic. Love has been
reduced to private feelings of coziness by many young people,
or love has been dispersed into a vague obscurantism which
provides an umbrella under which one can do almost anything and claim to have applied gospel love. It is difficult,
for example, to tell the difference between Joseph Fletcher's
view of love in his *Situation Ethics* and Erich Fromm's view
in his *The Art of Loving*. The former supposedly represents
a distinctive Christian position, the latter an avowedly hu-
manistic-secular view. But regardless of the problem of a
Christian vs. a secular view, surely everyone has the responsibility to be as precise as possible about what one means by
the concept "love." Otherwise one is riding on the wave of
popular appeal but only adding to the chaos of misunder-
standing and misuse.

2. As with some of the virtues of natural law, so with this
virtue of situationalism: Its flexibility and adaptability can
often become its weaknesses. An overemphasis on adaptability to unusual crisis problems—as is often the case with
Fletcher—can lead one to ignore the standard virtues of

honesty, integrity, property rights, and many relatively moral customs. Of course one is not going to tell the secret police where the brilliant Uncle Dudley is; to tell a plausible lie here is "the loving thing to do." But from this incident, one should not conclude that honesty is useless, or that honest persons are just used hypocritically by the Establishment. What needs to be stressed is this: The very fact that some standard ethical principles have to be compromised or flexibly ignored is what makes the problem a crisis, something unusual, or a "situation." In any case, one still needs to be reminded as to what are the principles one is being flexible about or adapting. Overemphasis on the action can lead to neglect of the virtue, just as overemphasis on the principle of the virtue can lead to neglect of action.

3. A third weakness of the love ethic is that it gives little clue as to how one gets "from here to there." That is to say, one seldom knows how one perceives the nature of Christ's love and then translates that into some specific moral decision and action. The importance of that information becomes enormous when one realizes that such a process is also filled with one's own motives, feelings, biases, desires, and sin. Love, therefore, is inevitably going to be infected, corrupted, changed, or thinned out.

Even more dangerous is the assumption that because one starts with Christian love he will also end up with its pure and relevant application. This inevitable self-righteousness has been ubiquitously laid bare by Reinhold Niebuhr in his writings. In sum, there is a mystifying mixture of love and sin, ambiguous human emotions, and complex external situations in almost all ethical dilemmas. Therefore, it simply will not do to pass over lightly the process of getting "from here to there," from love to action.

4. Another commonly noted weakness in the situational ethic is its unchecked individualism. While Fletcher is right in pointing out that precisely because the individual Christian is "free" to apply love, he is thereby responsible and ac-

countable. As a general statement this is true and necessary; but what it omits to answer is the question: To whom or to what is one accountable? The obvious answer, of course, is that one is responsible to God. But saying that is not enough either. For what does that statement mean? How—concretely —is one accountable to Ultimate Reality? And even if that is explained more clearly, are we not also responsible to other people, to society, to mankind? If this is true, does this responsibility not also have to be specified and detailed? Without such clarification, one is always able to justify himself by asserting that one "did it out of love"—as if that settled the matter. However relative individual and social standards are thought to be, some yardsticks must have at least temporary claim upon us if we are to be genuinely accountable to our fellowman. Otherwise a vague principle of an abstract God will let us off too easily.

5. Lastly, an apparently minor point should be noted among the weaknesses—a point we shall try to develop later. It is the problem of the teachability of an ethic, of the ease or difficulty of transferring the ethic to successive generations. I would argue that the highly individualistic nature of the ethic, its abstract assumption of love, and the mystifying complexity of its application make this ethic very difficult to teach or to transmit. The obvious answer is that what is transferred is not an autonomous body of knowledge (as in natural law) but a contagious life-style. While there is clearly merit in this rejoinder, I would still argue that somewhere, somehow, sometime one has to put concrete substance, rational understanding, and order into the "style."

From the Protestant situational love ethic let us extract and contribute to the ethical synthesis the primary emphasis of Christian love as the heart of the ethic, the need for adequate secular "situational" knowledge, and the flexible application of love to life.

Chapter
III

THEIR COMMON FEET OF CLAY

As all students of ethics know, any Christian ethical system is based upon various theological positions. While most ethicists acknowledge their theological source, many ignore or pass over too lightly other influential doctrines. On the whole, Rome is better than Geneva in spelling out the theological dogmas that are involved. Nevertheless, more doctrinal work needs to be done in areas such as epistemology, the nature of man, and the Holy Spirit. There are radical differences between Rome and Geneva on these three theological problems. Catholics and Protestants each need to give these problems further explication within their respective households of faith, but also in consultation and dialogue with each other. In our next chapter we shall try to offer suggestions for a rapprochement in these basic areas. Meanwhile, it is essential that ethicists of both traditions acknowledge the need for doing their theological homework.

1. *The Problem of Casuistry.* Although the practice of "casuistry" has a bad name in some Protestant circles, it is obvious to all ethicists that both Rome and Geneva engage in it. Whatever the word may have meant historically at any given moment, it has always, at best, meant the rational and intuitive process of applying general principles of ethics to a particular problem and deciding just how much circumstances alter cases.

As far as the process goes, it does not matter whether the "general" principle is pure agape or some broad principle like justice. Casuistry is the effort of man to apply (or make relevant) the abstract to the specific. And whether one uses only "law" (reason), or only "love" (intuition), or both, it is the process that is significant, not the facilities used.

In general, the dominant tool in casuistry has been reason, or logic. And casuistry received such a bad name partly because of the extensive and exhaustive exercises in definitions, qualifications, and explanations of exceptions, modifications, and other extenuating circumstances, etc., by those who practiced it. Even the incomparable Thomas Aquinas is difficult to read, and it is because of his precise logic and orderly argumentation, seen especially in the famous ethical section of his *Summa*. But he is lucidity unparalleled when one compares him with later writers on natural law and moral theology. It was indeed servants in the house of Rome who gave casuistry its bad name: they logic-chopped while men cried for ethical bread. But outside of Rome, the same abuse is also discernible. Better than a sleeping pill is Mortimer's chapter on justice in his book on moral theology.[4] Or even so staunch a Protestant as Paul Ramsey can "make like a moral theologian" when he writes: "But at a minimum it should be said that in addition to 'exempting conditions' and 'qualifying conditions' we need such designations as 'explaining principles' or 'explanatory qualifications' in order to comprise all the elements within the nature and the 'logic' by which we move along the spectrum from the most general ethical principles to more specific ones." And again: "On the face of it, this looks like a program for squeezing out the role of prudence in the subsumption of cases, or, rather, of supplanting the function of practical wisdom by some 'definite action-rule.' This would seem to require *per impossibile* a principle or rule governing the *application* of one's last specification to particular cases as the only way of showing that particular choice should always accord with some definite rule or principle or moral-*species* term." [5]

While the above example could be dismissed as "another Ramseyism," it is still an observable fact that no matter who writes or uses casuistry in any detail in the field of moral theology and natural law, he has to use many definitions and explanations of great detail. And while this must be done, should be done, and is being done, nevertheless it represents an occupational hazard. The weakness is that one can obscure a clear principle by defining 17 different exceptions which could occur under 9 variable conditions whose relevance could be mitigated by 4 possible circumstances. One versed in logic and ratiocination can draw upon several virtuous principles and note many variables and thereby justify almost any action. Again, if one scholar does not like the terms previously used (e.g., "primary principles" and "secondary principles," "prescriptive," or "illuminative"), he can always come up with new labels. Some of the latest are "rule-agapism," "act-agapism," and "koinonia ethics." These *can* be helpful, but they may also tend to obscure the meaning, depending on the author. In short, casuistry—like many sharp tools—can cut both ways, and whether it clarifies or obscures depends on the user. The trouble with noting this obvious generality is that everyone agrees with it, and each almost always thinks it is the other fellow who is the misuser. Both Roman and non-Roman moral theologians are still offering moral minutiae of boring redundance.

If the above generalization is true of Rome, it is equally applicable to Geneva. While many Protestants point out the misuses of casuistry, we often delude ourselves into thinking we do not use it at all, and are therefore free from its evils. The fact is, we do engage in the process and are equally culpable in its misuse. For example, it would seem that Fletcher in his *Situation Ethics* has done away with all casuistry by asserting: "Love decides there and then." [6] And while he

clearly believes in the use of reason and principle (so long
as they are advisory maxims only), he nevertheless applies
Christian love to particular problems. The process of application *is* casuistry no matter how much or how little reason is
used. And Fletcher is no better than anyone else in his use
and misuse. Sometimes his application is fairly clear, i.e., the
chief determining factor seems to be "beneficial effect on the
doer"; at other times this utility principle is abandoned.
When it is, we are not told how or why. (For a detailed discussion of this weakness in Fletcher see chapter 7 of Ramsey's
Deeds and Rules.)[7]

As for the rest of us who are in and out of the house of
Geneva, we cannot pick on Fletcher. For, as we confessed
earlier, most of us are really never quite sure how we apply
our general principle, how we get "from here to there." If
Rome is largely guilty of overdefinition and overexplanation,
Geneva is guilty of underdefinition and underexplanation. We
tend to say: We're expressing love; there's no reasoning in
our nice, free, Christian love ethic. Such a claim is an arrogant
illusion. We apply love but do not spell out how we do it, and
that is perhaps even more obscurantist. It is to the great
credit of Paul Ramsey (and others, such as William Frankena)
that he keeps on writing and spelling out helpful guides and
descriptions of constructive casuistry, and challenging the rest
of us to do so. We owe it to him and to the households of
both traditions to supply a few issues of our own!

2. *The Easy Conscience.* After an ethical decision or moral
action, both Rome and Geneva leave man with an easy conscience. In the systems of moral theology and natural law at
their best, the ethicists figure out the complexities of a given
problem, check out the relevant principles, infuse them and
the doer with love, apply it to the whole situation, and then
give the verdict: this is best, that is valid, or right. Presumably,
one then does the deed and does so with the assurance of
righteousness or virtue.

Similarly in Protestant ethics, one gets in tune with love,

analyzes the ambiguity of the situation, applies love concretely and then decides that this action is "the loving thing to do," or "doing reality" (Bonhoeffer). Here too, after the act, one can feel justified.

Now the obvious question is, Why should an easy conscience be regarded as a weakness? Have we not had too much "Puritan guilt" already? Were not D. C. Mackintosh and, more recently, Paul Ramsey right in attacking Reinhold Niebuhr's insistence on choosing "the lesser of two evils"? Their point was: Why not stress that the choice involves doing the best good possible? Surely our culture has wallowed in sin and guilt long enough, and the psychiatrist's couches have been laden with guilt-ridden patients. So why is there now an attack against a justified and easy conscience?

My response will be stated first as a dogmatic assertion and then, it is hoped, evidence will be offered for its veracity. The proposition: Any moral system that leaves man with an easy conscience will inevitably lead to the corruption of both the person and the system. Let us examine the evidence.

First, the role of ideals within and outside the church provides us with many empirical examples. If one sees the church as the Kingdom of God on earth, the vehicle of the Holy Spirit, it is very easy to get defensive and idolatrous about the visible church. Judging from its behavior, the church has never really believed that it might have to lose its visible life in order to save it. On the contrary, the church has made all kinds of compromises in order to survive intact. For example, the Russian Orthodox Church is permitted to exist so long as it guarantees, if not approval of the Communist Party, at least moral silence on the state's activities. Similarly, the Greek Orthodox Church has recently been granted millions from the Greek colonels for new church buildings in return for a deafening silence about their dictatorship. The papal silence in World War II is still within memory, and the churches (especially the Protestant churches) did little about the Vietnam war. There are always plausible reasons for moral compromise and silence—e.g., since layman and clergy are divided, a church cannot claim to be the voice or the representative of all members. But quite apart from the pro and con on Vietnam, certainly there were means and methods used—by both sides—that warranted some prophetic notice and judgment. So with racial justice, the one brave foray into actual appropriations for programs for blacks (in the Episcopal Church) was met with a noticeable decrease in lay giving. Then the word had to go out: Soften the talk, mute the noise, draw back on the program, don't upset things anymore!

Thus, in the name of the prophets and the Christ, the church has persuaded the world that its ideals and institutions are so true and so valuable that they must be preserved at all costs. The secular world in general agrees that so long as one is pursuing a noble ideal or virtue almost anything goes en route. The Pentagon Papers reveal this phenomenon with pathetic clarity. The volumes, along with fairly extensive personal interviews by this writer in 1963–1964, show that the top policymakers were men of goodwill, honest and hardworking men who wanted to do the best thing for their country. Their fatal flaw was their blind allegiance to the ideal of anticommunism. The basic assumption was that almost any means to defeat the Communists was justifiable. There was no cabal of evil men rejoicing in evil. These were men as morally good as any of the rest of us. So how does one account for the vastly evil means that were used? How does one get in the frame of mind which calls for the invention of a bomb (i.e., the splinter bomb) that maims but does not kill?

Part of the answer has to be that one believes in the obvious virtue of anticommunism. This is combined with good motives of working for one's country and working long and hard at it. And the goals are also virtuous: freedom and democracy. Now contrast this with the obvious evil of Communism, the horrible terror of the Viet Cong assassinations, and therefore our inevitable need to stop them. The moral balance sheet comes out very favorably for us. Our only morally questionable area seems to be a few means—but even those are mostly caused by the Viet Cong guerrilla tactics. So what is so evil about us?

Most policymakers sincerely believed something like the above. This syndrome also helps one understand why it took them so long to see the vast evils we were committing. The most obvious cause of such evils was that we were not winning. Other causes were the effective, subtle ones of screening out any evidence of both failure and wrongdoing—a very natural (sinful!) thing to do. The frequent "inspection visits" to Vietnam by Secretary of Defense Robert McNamara and others were always exercises in "success." What general or commander is going to emphasize his failures to his boss? It was the press and McNamara's adamant insistence on "more evidence" which finally surfaced most of the evils of our means and methods. And gradually most of the policymakers on the second level changed. There were many other factors involved which we cannot go into in this book. Suffice it to point out here that *one* basic ingredient was this pursuit of the great ideal that enables man to feel righteous, yet in the very process to commit terrible evils. As in the crucifixion Jesus was not killed by evil men, so also in this war relatively good men did evil things in the name of the good and in the belief that they were doing good. When one is pursuing or defending the good, how easy it is to justify the less obvious evil means, particularly when the enemy appears to be so flagrantly evil. Only toward the end of our Vietnam engagement did we realize that over one million innocent villagers had been killed by our "lesser of two evils" methods, and so consciences became uneasy.

Yet, a few years later, consciences were again at ease. For —as shown by columnist Jack Anderson's publication of secret government reports—in the policy decisions about which side to support in the Indo-Pakistani war, the slaughter of the East Pakistanis in Bangladesh (over 400,000 dead, plus 10 million refugees) was not even mentioned or considered—so single-mindedly were we playing the anticommunist game.

The other common method for retaining an easy conscience is to make a god of Realism. Thus it is said: "Rome wasn't built in a day; you have to be practical." Or again: "A man has to eat, institutions must survive, so you have to be realistic." We are all familiar with these slogans and the efficient moral compromise they represent. Readers can suggest their own examples. But here again the point is not that ideals and practical realism are evil; they are not. The point is that we use them as justification for retaining an easy conscience. And when realism and idealism are used in that manner and under the aegis of the church, one has a veritable edifice of righteousness.

The realist, secular or Christian, is notorious for becoming tougher and tougher as he becomes more efficient. He gets things done and we could not live without him. But sometimes it would appear that when vast power is available, we cannot live with him either.

In summary then, I believe a case can be made for speaking of the dangers of an easy conscience. What we shall have to do in the course of the next chapter is to spell out the critical difference between destructive guilt and creative moral uneasiness. For it is this latter ingredient which seems to me to be needed in both Christian ethical traditions if their synthesis is to be tolerable.

Chapter
IV

THE THEOLOGICAL FORM OF THE SYNTHESIS

Competent persons will have to work out more fully and more adequately the deeper implications of the theological problems involved in the synthesis we have proposed. This small book can only point up what I regard as the seven essential bases for the synthesis.

The Theological Ingredients

1. *God.* Much contemporary theology has rightly emphasized the presence of God in and around the life of the individual. The availability and nearness of God to both the man of faith and the seeker is a frequent theme. This emphasis should be continued as well as refined.

An emphasis that needs to be revived, however, is the prophetic tradition of affirming God as also the Lord of history. Granted all the difficulties of "discerning the signs of the times" and the dangers of equating God with historical movements, nevertheless every one of us needs a strong awareness that there is a moral order to history, that nations cannot run amok without some form of judgment occurring, and that it is not oneself or the nation who is the Lord, but the mighty Creator. More specifically, this means that somebody should be proclaiming that perhaps both the Viet Cong and the

United States are being judged for their arrogance and terror; that our travail (and theirs) is a just judgment on our immorality; and that the blood of the millions of refugees and innocent natives not only outlines the tragic dimension of life but also the depth and breadth of our guilt.

In the present ecological crisis someone should remind us once again about the orders of nature and creation—that "whatever a man sows, that he will also reap." A contemporary translation could easily read: "As we throw refuse, so shall we reap pollution." The evidence of order in nature is mounting and becoming increasingly clear. But similar clarity and discernment is lacking in the historical scene where more theoretical and specific work is needed. Otherwise, patriotism and politics will increase in their imaginings that they can rule history and ruin people with impunity. Incredible as it sounds, one United States senator seriously announced during the Korean war that if as a result of our atomic bombing of the Chinese they retaliated by a full-scale invasion of South Korea, he "would personally apologize." How comforting and paternal! To revive an old cliché: we and the nation's leaders "need to have the fear of God put into us."

Thus it seems to me that we need to sensitize our households to the awareness that God does work in history not only in and through individuals and nature but also in major historical events. We need a renewed sense that some moral evils such as racism and exploitation of the poor, and even some wars, are not only offenses against man but also offenses against God and his creation; they are against the very nature of things—against reality itself.

2. *Christ.* The relation of various views of the nature and purpose of Christ also rightly concern scholar and layman alike. As noted previously,[8] James Gustafson has given us a fine study showing how particular views tend to produce particular ethical tendencies. And earlier, H. Richard Niebuhr gave us a similar study but related to cultural stances.[9] What is now needed, it seems to me, is first to assert the rather obvi-

ous point that *all* views of Christ's work are necessary; that it is fruitless to try to assert the primacy or superiority of one emphasis over another. What is to be gained by trying to avow that Christ should be our model for ethical behavior, while neglecting to take account of his justifying or sacrificial work, or vice versa? By what right does one try to limit or confine Christ to one category or action?

It seems, therefore, equally obvious that the fundamental issue is how one decides which interpretation of Christ is most applicable to a particular ethical decision and moral action. Or to put it in Niebuhrean terms: given a moral problem such as a guaranteed annual income bill or an ecological measure, shall we try to approach the problem as Christians against our culture, or as sanctifiers of it, or in an ambiguous tension? And how does one decide which approach or emphasis to take? What is the principle by which one makes such a decision? These seem to be the really basic questions to be worked out. I shall attempt to suggest possible answers in the next chapter. Meanwhile, the point is: we must be sure that we have the full Christ present and available; our real task is to learn how to emphasize now *this* aspect of him, and now *that*.

3. *The Holy Spirit.* With many people claiming the Holy Spirit as the source of their wisdom and the sanctifier of their moral action, this doctrine surely needs redefining. But why must we insist on only one definition or restatement? Granted the many misuses of concepts of the Holy Spirit, could we not agree upon two or three basic emphases? The classical Biblical view that "where two or three are gathered in my name, there am I" (the Spirit in the church) is obviously essential. But so, too, is the later formulation that the Spirit can work through individuals, and in other "mysterious ways." While we cannot put limits on how the Spirit works, perhaps we can at least agree that man should be cautious about claiming his own identification with it. Jesus warned us especially not to claim too much righteousness for our supposedly virtuous

deeds. "When you have done all that is commanded you, say, 'We are unworthy servants.'" (Luke 17:10.)

The two basic points here, I think, are to keep ourselves open to the workings of the Spirit and to make no claims beforehand that we have been chosen as a vehicle. If later on, in hindsight, we find some evidence that warrants our awareness of being such an instrument, then render thanks to God rather than adulation of institution or self.

4. *Human Nature.* Various views of man, like views of Christ, affect one's ethics and morals. It has been argued in an earlier chapter that some estimates of man's goodness are too high. Some Roman Catholic theologians assume a too-easy infusion of grace, which seems to eliminate any ambiguity in moral motivation. Similarly, some Protestant theologians seem to assert that the man of faith can rather easily know what it is to be human, and how to translate that knowledge into specific moral decisions. Sometimes both Rome and Geneva seem to feel that even if some individuals are not particularly graceful, the church somehow can overcome moral ambiguity and know and do the really righteous thing.

Needless to say, the secular world, as well as many within the church, are not impressed with such claims and rightly ask for the evidences of such sterling and unambiguous righteousness. What is needed, it seems to me, is the reassertion of Augustine's insistence that sin is the corruption of goodness. We need *not* have a revival of wallowing in sin. But surely we do need to achieve a proper blend, a balance of the awareness of the mix of good and evil in all that we do. And it may be that we should tilt this balance now and then—now emphasizing the good possibilities that are available, then emphasizing how easily this good can be misused and corrupted. We need to remind the optimists of the subtleties of sin, even as we need to remind the pessimists of the power available to do good.

The problem of reason and sin also needs to be restudied and the extreme claims reexamined. It should be possible for

Geneva to admit that formal reason can know some of the formal principles of ethics. Empirically speaking, isn't it true that man "knows" that justice is better than injustice, that love is better than hate, and that murders shall not be condoned? But is it not also possible for Rome to admit that reason can be corrupted by sin and overwhelmed by egoism and passion? The danger of Rome's view of reason has been its claim that it can equate specific rational application of divine law to human morals. Or, conversely, when a specific problem arises, Rome has often asserted that it knows what the eternal or divine law is. A more profound Augustinian doctrine of sin is needed here. The lack of a sense of discontinuity or sinful ambiguity between man's reason and God's will on specifics has been and still is one of the chief causes of serious difference on issues such as abortion, celibacy, and euthanasia. This writer has the temerity to suggest that Rome should keep its insistence on reason as a valid point of contact between man and God in certain ethical and general areas, but that it should also be ready to concede that even this capacity can be corrupted. Therefore it must be careful about claims of knowing God's will or natural law. Geneva ought to be able to acknowledge the validity of reason and the essential need for it in any ethical system, and at the same time to stop claiming that inspiration or prayer or "existential awareness" frees one from ambiguity, corruption, and sin. The more precise formulations of the relation of sin, reason, grace, knowledge, ethical principles, and the like, I assign to tomorrow's young theologians!

Meanwhile, if our suggested blend of goods and evils on all levels in man is somewhere nearly right, this leads again to our demand for a new concept of the uneasy conscience. In the last chapter we tried to establish the need for such a concept, but concluded that we must show why such a view would be creative rather than neurotic. To this we now turn.

The choice of the word "uneasy" is designed to distinguish this concept from most forms of guilt. By "uneasy" I mean it to convey the recognition that moral motives and moral situations are mixtures of good and evil. I believe it is essential that we remain aware of the evil present in most of our doings. Without such awareness, it is so very easy to slide into feelings of self-righteousness and moral comfort. Yet, in contrast to self-hating guilt, there is also the awareness of the presence of good in both motive and situation. Uneasiness should imply neither self-righteousness nor destructive guilt. I mean it to reflect the combination.

To be sure, we may not always be able to calculate the precise ratio of good and evil in motive or action. It is rare, if not impossible, to detect a 58 percent good in a motive, a 26 percent egoism factor, and thus a 16 percent neutral area. Nevertheless, it is fairly accurate to assume some mixture in our motives, and perhaps with the aid of "right reason" discern an approximate 60–40 percent ratio in a specific situation. In any case, the point is the need to have a rather regular awareness of our continual moral mix. This should keep us sensitive to the presence of *both* good and evil in our moral living.

In a basic sense, of course, this is really not a new idea; it has been present in the Christian tradition from the beginning. It is perhaps best found in the doctrines of justification by faith and sanctification by the Holy Spirit.

5. *Justification by Faith.* In addition to the other uses and meanings of this dogma, I would hope that it could also be used to deal with the uneasy conscience. Historically this dogma was born out of the awareness of the moral gap between "Be ye perfect" and the fact of our sinful condition, which would obviously prevent us from being perfect, at least in any moral achievement sense. Thus, as we all know, we are justified—accepted in the household—not by good works, but by our faith relationship with God. The human parent analogy has always seemed to me to be the most exact and accurate illustration: our love for our children is *not* dependent upon their achieving some high level of moral good-

ness. One cannot expect a five-year-old to act like a twenty-five-year-old. To condemn a child morally by adult standards is indeed to introduce destructive and helpless guilt into his personality. On the other hand, we do not ignore his breaking the window. There is moral education involved: we try to help the child see that playing ball with others is a good pastime, but breaking windows is not. The mixture of good and bad is made known—but made known within the context of ethically discerning love and faithful commitment one to another. So the child is accepted, understood, and justified by his relationship (faith).

Justification by faith, at its best, can be the producer and maintainer of the creative uneasy conscience. It helps us to acknowledge the struggles we have with good and evil both inside of us and in the external world. It enables us to face up to this fact because we know we are understood and accepted by our Father. Thus, rather than trying to hide our moral failures or rationalize them away, we are encouraged by the loving relationship to face up to the mixtures, understand the subtleties, and therefore to find help in dealing with them.

The rite of confession at its best is also one concrete method of helping the conscience to be aware and to be creatively uneasy. At its worst, however, and in common practice, the Saturday confession tends to deal with obvious and small sins and also, through minor penances, tends to induce an easy conscience. But properly used, confessions can be one helpful method for maintaining and educating the uneasy conscience. Another kind of help is found in the following doctrine.

6. *Sanctification by the Holy Spirit.* The obvious ethical relevance in this doctrine is the reception of more power to love ("to do good"). On the whole, Rome and Canterbury have long seen this point and practiced it. Geneva, on the other hand, has often reduced the doctrine to individual inspiration. Granted that all traditions have often misused or made extreme claims about how the Holy Spirit affects moral action, nevertheless, it is an essential source of our ethical life.

What we need to emphasize, I think, are three basic items: First, sanctification is *one* way by which one can receive the power to love. This is a critical factor related to our doctrine of man. If it is true that the kind of love Jesus revealed and called for is *not* naturally present in man, that this love is from God, *is* God's love, then man needs to receive this love. Sanctification is one of the chief resources for this kind of love. Second, it needs to be stressed, in addition to the various individual relationships with God, that group experience with God's spirit and love is equally essential. Here again a balance between the emphasis of Protestant individualism and Roman church "tradition" is needed; not one or the other, but both. And each has much to learn from the other. But at this juncture in our culture, with the outward decline of churches, plus the emphasis on private individualism, experience in the corporate life of the church is much needed. This point leads us to a discussion of the third item—liturgy.

Liturgy has been one of the most effective media for spiritual renewal; but like the churches, much of the liturgy is archaic, or seems to be. Experiments with new liturgies or mild reforms of the old have not, as yet, been successful—largely because it is obvious to date that there is no one right liturgy. How can the Holy Spirit be confined to only one type of ritual or one set of symbols? Is it not desirable, then, to continue the traditional forms for those who want them, and at the same time to press on to new forms and ways of corporate worship and liturgy?

Regardless of what is retained or discovered, however, our crucial point is to reaffirm the doctrine of sanctification by the Holy Spirit as *one* essential method by which a person can receive new power to love.

7. *Christian Love.* We have accused others of failing to define what they mean by their use of the word "love." So now it is my duty to say what I mean when I speak of Christian love.

It is sometimes helpful to begin by saying what Christian love is *not*. It is not, for example, the normal, natural, prudential love (I'll love you if you'll love me). Christ asked: "If you love those who love you, . . . what more are you doing than others?" Christian love is not a bargaining or conditional love (e.g., If you agree to handle the children and the house, then I'll take care of the finances and support). Nor is Christian love the natural, romantic, "cozy" love portrayed in many movies and sought for by adolescents. Nor is it, finally, the vague but pervasive semierotic love that not only expresses itself through sex but also seeks romantic ecstasy in nature, experience, life, and ideals à la D. H. Lawrence and N. O. Brown.

From a Christian point of view, none of these loves are bad; they are quite natural and normal. But Christian love is something else. What is it, then? It is best exemplified by Jesus, who shows us that God's love is a seeking out, an outreach (the parable of the lost sheep), an enormously sensitive and tender caring ("Consider the lilies of the field . . ."), a readiness to forgive and to renew ("How often . . . shall I forgive?" "Seventy times seven"), an eagerness to reconcile and restore ("Be reconciled to your brother"), a readiness to sacrifice ("Let him take up his cross and follow me"), a just sternness ("Go, and do not sin again"), and a willingness to suffer ("O Jerusalem, Jerusalem, killing the prophets . . .").

Paul added other descriptive notes in his famous chapter 13 in I Corinthians, where he describes Christian love as unconditional in that it seeks no reward, is not proud, does not envy, has the sympathetic capacity to share and to identify with someone else, "delights in the truth," and can bear all things.

Looking at the New Testament as a whole, we note other most significant aspects of Christian love. There is the Johannine account of the resurrected Jesus thrice commanding the disciples to feed and tend his sheep. This would seem to suggest not only personal ethics but some kind of social ethics. My favorite synonym for "love" is the word "caring." Christian love cares about what happens to people. This word and its connotation seems to me to suggest the widest possible concerns and therefore lays the groundwork for both personal and social ethics. It should help overcome the narrow view that one should offer only spiritual help to the poor but not material aid. Caring about persons would include being concerned about their physical as well as their mental and spiritual well-being. And the expression of our concern could take many forms—political and economic as well as personal— through prayer and hope.

But perhaps most uniquely significant are Jesus' sayings and actions concerning love of one's enemies: "pray for those who persecute you," turn the other cheek, go the second mile. It is Jesus' love-of-enemies concept which makes it clear to me why Christian love is not naturally present in human nature. There is a key difference between high humanism and Christian faith. I believe it is empirically quite demonstrable that man does not have the kind of love Jesus revealed. For example, if someone hits, robs, or exploits us, our *natural* reaction is to fight back. It is also quite natural to hate the person. We do *not* find ourselves down on our knees praying for that person's good. It is altogether normal and human to want to retaliate in kind. Therefore, Jesus' command to love our enemies asks of us an unnatural act. We do not have that kind of love present in us. That is why we need power from beyond ourselves; that is why Christian love is from God, not man. Or, to put it another way, if we were able to love the way Jesus asks us to do, who would need God? We could do it on our own.

Thus, love of enemies as demonstrated by Jesus is the most dramatic characteristic of Christian love and one which sets it apart from natural human love. It is this fact which also underlies the earlier affirmation that the one and only absolute in Christian ethics is Christian love. Since God is the Absolute, it follows that his love is our only ethical absolute;

all else is relative to that. The significance of this point will be expanded upon in the next chapter.

Summary

First, I do believe it is possible for Rome and Geneva to agree essentially on all the theological ingredients so far described in this chapter. There may be better ways of stating a doctrine, making different analogies, and *varying* the emphasis as needed. But, basically, it seems to me that general agreement in the substance and form of theology is now possible, and in many cases, already actual.

Secondly, I find that the one key area of disagreement is the nature of authority. While that problem spills over into several areas such as apostolic succession and "tradition," in the area of ethics and morals the critical issue is the magisterium. For Rome, the magisterium will settle authoritatively any really critical moral or ethical dilemma. For Geneva, there is no absolute settlement. Protestants have many checks and balances and illuminations, such as the Bible, the church, the Holy Spirit, prophets, individual conscience, and the weight of experience. But none of these resources, nor all of them together, can provide an absolute answer. For Geneva, this is precisely one reason why we have to walk by faith, not sight —ethically and theologically.

Finally, with both Rome and Geneva now studying seriously and anew the problem of authority on all levels, I do not see that this present impasse need prevent the ethical synthesis.[10] The problem is an unhappy danger area; there will be continued tension and disagreement, even sharp divergence at times, as there is now. But given our other wide basic agreements plus the renewed goodwill in both households, I for one am ready for the making of the ethical synthesis.

Chapter
V

THE ETHICAL FORM OF THE SYNTHESIS

The ethical ingredients of this profound synthesis need further development. I have already stressed the primary essential of Christian love, but let it be stated again that Christian love is *the* basis of our ethics. Now, *after* that, we turn to other necessary ingredients, the first of which is natural law.

Natural Law

Under this broad title we have already suggested a review of the nature of reason, its limits and its corruption by sin. At the same time we will continue to insist on its fullest use at all times, particularly in *how* ethics are to be applied, the subject to be dealt with in the next chapter. Now it is imperative that we call for a renewed look at the meaning of the word "nature" in "natural law."

The basic assumption behind natural law ethics is that there are rational structures within the natural process, that these can be discerned by human reason, and that these orders are morally necessary. Thus, it has long been asserted that such "realities" as the state, the family, the rule of no murder within the tribe, are all "natural moral realities." As such, they are observable by any rational man and therefore have universal validity and application.

With the great increase in the study of anthropology and with the availability of worldwide information on many cultures, the universality of most "natural laws" has been challenged. There seems to be at least a genuine debate on universal vs. relative cultural practices. In my judgment, there is evidence for at least an ethical rational morality that is nearly universal. For example, it would seem to me that the following assertions are a tenable rational position: Some kind of state is necessary; some kind of family is essential; some kind of prohibition of torture of children and innocents is imperative; some kind of rules about ecological behavior are required; and some guiding principles are requisite for us to deal with various psychological facts about the damage that hate can cause.

These statements reflect general but nonetheless real structures of "life" or "reality" or "nature." They are close to what the Reformers meant when they used the term "orders of creation." The inference is clear: there are some structures embedded in life. If a minimal quality of life is to be maintained, these natural realities must be followed. Differences enter the picture when we define these structures and particularly when we devise specific ways of abiding by such "orders." Thus, we can say that it is natural and rational and moral to have a state, a government—i.e., this is a universal ethical structure. What *kind* of state it should be and what *form* it should take are highly relative matters and should be so.

But how does this answer the objections of the anarchist? The assertion of the moral need of a state does not make it immoral for various individuals to seek to live without a government. There is room for the hermit, the small communes, and other nonconforming individuals or groups. Our universal "state" principle is *not* our absolute. It is a general order which does not exclude other "orders"—even individual privacy. But if our absolute is Christian love, as we have previously stated, and if we wish to put it into practice, *then* some kind of state is necessary for a practical application of love. One might desire the minimal type of social order, especially in the face of our present vast bureaucracies. Even so, *some* order is necessary. For example, if an individual or a small commune wants education or medicine, those two items alone require some kind of state, for both enterprises depend upon shared and organized knowledge and equipment as well as communication and distribution. So if I am to express love concretely to someone who is both ignorant and ill, I will need some minimal social, governmental structure to provide the goods.

Our point here is to indicate that in arguing for the existence of natural, rational, moral, and therefore universal ethical principles we are not ruling out exceptions or alternative options. It might be helpful to make a distinction between the "universal" and the "absolute." The Absolute for Christians is God, and his love through Christ is the absolute for ethics. "Absolute" means here "the highest, the top reality, the greatest, *the* source for judgment and evaluation." The universal, on the other hand, while less than and subject to the absolute, nevertheless means something that is generally applicable and true. A universal ethical principle such as "You shall not murder" is not made invalid because there are or may be exceptions. The exceptions do not come from an opposite universal ethical principle such as "It is morally good to murder." The exceptions, if any, come only from that which is higher, namely, the absolute. Or if there is a series of general principles and two of them conflict, then one has to make clear what is *the* yardstick, *the* principle of selection. Thus, in the case of an ill, pregnant mother, the classic dilemma arises as to which life should be saved: the life of the mother, or that of the baby. The key issue here is: What is the yardstick by which one decides which of the two valid but conflicting principles should be used? "Thou shalt save life," or "Thou shalt not take life"? Let us not wiggle out of this dilemma by calling the baby a fetus, or the mother a demented psychotic. And let us not soften the situation by saying, "Permit the doctor to decide that nature should take its course so that 'there will be no intention to destroy life.'" Let us be bold and difficult—as life often is. Let us say that the choice is either to remove the premature baby from the uterus and thereby effectively kill it and thus save the mother's life, or not to treat the mother's illness but let her struggle on until the baby is old enough to be saved by either caesarian section or delivery, leaving the mother so weak and debilitated that she cannot live. Just how does one decide? What is the determining principle or criterion? Obviously, there are several possibilities on which to base one's choice: the capacity for producing life; the quality of individual life; the contribution of one life to the many affected by it; the potential for new quality of life; new versus old—the newer supposedly being the more valuable. It is easy to see how one could use one or more of these reasons and come to opposite conclusions. If one wants to save the baby, one emphasizes potential and new life. If the mother's life is to be saved, one urges the capacity and the quality and need for life now.

What needs to be stressed here is that these are all general principles, related to nature, rationally definable, but also often in conflict with each other. Hence, the critical decision is the priority value that is present in or behind or above the system. In the above example, *the* determining value for me would be first Christian love applied to both mother and baby. Second, the quality of that love would require a distinction, namely, that the baby is not fully capable of receiving or giving much love, nor does it need full love. By contrast, the mother needs all the depth and richness of love. In terms of quality, she has love, needs love, and can also share and extend love to others. Another way of putting it is to say that the baby's quality of life and love is potential; the mother's is "real" and actual. Therefore, the next value assumption is that effective love is best given to real persons rather than potential ones. The tragedy of the loss of the child is also clearly noted and affirmed. This is an evil, a moral one, and we are responsible, not for the situation but for the choice we make. We do not claim that it was a perfectly obvious moral choice, for it was not. But presumably we have made clear the principles involved, why we chose this and not that course. That is the key point.

Similarly I acknowledge that other Christians could have chosen other principles and come to the opposite conclusion. So long as they acknowledge their principles of selection, their value priority, and their moral blend of good and evil, I can have no quarrel with them.

But now the question remains: If two equally devout and rational Christians use rational principles and come to opposite conclusions, then where is the universal, where is the general natural, rational law? Do not two opposite conclusions invalidate any claim for universal reason? The answer is that there are many general principles, and the decision to favor one over the other is determined by the individual's application of love, plus his "situational" tactical estimate of which value should have priority. Thus, in the example of the baby vs. the mother, the same person might come to the opposite conclusion, depending on the situation. For instance, in heavily overpopulated India, one might easily decide in favor of the mother. But if one were in a sparsely populated island and progeny were desperately needed, assuming that other mothers were around to care for the child, one could conceivably decide in favor of saving the baby. In either case the application of love is the same, all the universal principles are the same, the use of reason and choice is the same; the only difference is the objective "situation." But in the earlier example of the doctor's decision, the selective difference would be the tactical and situational value judgment made concerning the same situation. Any difference between the decision of a doctor or a priest or a relative would be the individual's assessment of which principle should be operative at the time. And this judgment, in turn, would depend upon one's view of the nature of love, what aspect or values should be stressed, and upon the particular or existent situation.

In actual practice, the causes of the difference are many: e.g., ignorance, irrationality, blind loyalty. In addition, one may absolutize a principle such as "Never take a life under any circumstance." Or the opposite, "Always save the mother," could become one's absolute. I am not arguing the causes of actual instances but merely trying to establish the validity of universal ethical principles in spite of even formal cases of difference. The conclusion I have reached is that the difference ought to be due to subjective estimates of what is most needed in a given situation, of how love is most enhanced. Given human nature, such difference is often inevitable, but need not be destructive. More important, it is this kind of difference that overcomes the destructive types that are due to ignorance or absolutizing.

Finally, we must call attention to the fairly obvious but oft-forgotten fact that "crisis exceptions" to general principles do not invalidate them. It could even be argued that because dramatic and unique situations do exist they point up the fact of universality. Indeed, what makes an exception an exception is that it seldom occurs. If the exception becomes the rule, it is no longer unique: it is on its way to becoming a universal.

To sum up, we have been arguing that even from secular natural law ethics there is a basic contribution to be made to the proposed synthesis. That contribution is the historic view that there are some natural, rational, moral (or ethical) principles and orders of creation—i.e., the state, the family, the codes forbidding murder and torture, the improvement of the quality of life and love—which should be included in a Christian ethical system.

In the discussion of natural law ethics, I have extracted only the part I thought valid and helpful, namely, the broad ethical, "natural" principles. However, as we have seen, there are many weaknesses and dangers in most natural law systems. Hence it is important to emphasize the common danger of regarding nature as the whole of reality. This concept is partly contained in the cliché, "Whatever is natural is right." Many secular views adopt this assumption. The Kinsey reports of 1948 and 1953 reflect this view, and many people use the more recent Masters and Johnson findings in the same way—i.e., if empirical study shows that 75 percent of the people do this and that, the inference is that such behavior is natural and therefore right. Further, it is often argued that if value or moral judgments are contrary to nature, these morals are "outmoded or unnatural." I do not wish to go into a long debate on this philosophic concept, but suffice it to say that those making this assumption would also have to assert that the common cold is a moral good because 95 percent have it, or that cancer and heart attacks are good because they cause most deaths today.

We need not dwell on this kind of secular naturalism because Roman Catholic natural law concepts also fall into this error. Rome often argued that mechanical contraceptives are immoral because they are artificial; the rhythm method is defended purely on the grounds that it *is* natural. Such arguments clearly reflect the assumption that what is natural is right. Rome at its best knows better. That is why the concept of divine law was developed.

Divine Law

Rome has always known that all of nature is not necessarily good. There is disease; there is "earthquake, wind, and fire"; there are floods that kill and destroy. A mother superior's first warning to the novitiate nun is, "Remember, this [vocation] is *against* nature." Since nature is a mixture of order and disorder, creation and destruction, some facility is needed to discern the difference, to make the evaluation. Thus, Rome believes that one reason why this discernment is possible is that God has disclosed divine law through revelation and has disclosed his creation (or natural) law through man's basic being. Obviously there can be no contradiction between God's laws. In general, then, part of the divine law is reflected in natural law. This is why it is possible to discern the rational and the irrational in both nature and human nature. While divine law is for the most part known through faith, and natural law through reason, there is an overlap.[11] In any case, the chief point is to indicate that Rome is well aware of the danger of deifying nature. Whether one accepts its solution to this problem is something else. I for one cannot accept it because of the familiar epistemological weakness, i.e., the fact that man cannot know God's will precisely, either in its "divine" context, or in nature, or in man's own being. We can only see (know) as "through a glass darkly." However, for the sake of our proposed ethical synthesis, I wish to stress that Rome at its best knows that nature and natural law are not and cannot be self-sufficient sources for ethical principles, nor the means by which one selects the priority of principles.

The main points, then, which I am proposing are these: Geneva needs to be reminded that there are general structures in human life and natural process which are orderly and tend to make life creative. These structures are mostly discernible by reason. The value put on such "principles" is a mixture of human and divine cooperation, which makes it possible to assert that there *are* some general ethical principles that are essential to the moral life. None of them are absolute, but all have nearly universal relevance. Therefore, we do not go into most moral situations *de novo*. There is a lot of help around. Let us therefore pay attention to the structures of nature and the wisdom of man.

Similarly, Rome needs to be reminded that not all of nature is necessarily beneficial to man, nor its structures absolute in the value system. Theologians and ecclesiastical authorities need to recognize that the establishment of the priority of values and the selection of principles are not purely natural acts but theological choices. Beyond that, some need to exercise more humility in claiming to know God's will, and in identifying it with either human definition or natural process.

Nevertheless, the two traditions need not be forever separated in the problem of nature—for Geneva at its best, with its doctrine of creation and of reason as *a* gift of God can, it seems to me, form a useful alliance with Rome's chastened view of nature and reason.

Ideals

Another necessary ingredient in a Christian ethical system is the proper role and place for ideals. We have already noted the cultural phenomenon that in the United States of America most citizens believe that a set of noble ideals provides an adequate ethical system. And not a few church people turn the Christian faith into idealism when they extract a few lofty "teachings" concerned with love, kindness, or meekness. The assumption is that all that man needs are the right ideals, and then his job is to work hard to live up to them.

Some critics of ethical idealistic systems have thrown out ideals altogether. Or, love is substituted as *the* ideal, and other ideals are regarded as futile, irrelevant, and as sources of hypocrisy. I should like to revive the "middle axiom" concept of John C. Bennett, J. H. Oldham, and others and give a proper place to noble ideals. Just as the church adopted and used the ancient classical virtues of justice, prudence, temperance, and fortitude, I believe we should also include other and more recent ideals and virtues such as freedom, integrity, equality, liberation, trust, and honor.

How these ideals should be used in a Christian ethical system I will consider in the next chapter. But for now I want to assert the validity and usefulness of ideals in our proposed synthesis.

It seems to me that the proper and efficient use of noble human ideals is similar to the proper use of our natural law principles. Ideals can be used as guides to moral action and as signposts toward the goals to which we aspire. A nautical analogy is helpful: "Ideals are like stars; you will not succeed in touching them with your hands. But like the seafaring man . . . , following them you will reach your destiny." [12] More important, however, is John Macquarrie's point that what matters is not the particular bundle of ideals that one has, nor any unique claim for some special ideal. What is essential is the milieu, the theological home, the context in which the ideals are used.

Macquarrie writes: "What is distinctive in the Christian Ethic is not its ultimate goals or fundamental principles, for these are shared with all serious-minded people in whatever tradition they stand. The distinctive element is the special context within which the moral life is perceived. This special context includes the normative place assigned to Jesus Christ and his teaching—not, indeed, as a paradigm for external imitation, but rather as the criterion and inspiration for a style of life." [13]

It is at this point that the situational ethics school makes its most important contribution. Its way of stating Macquarrie's point is to assert that all ideals should be used under the aegis of Christian love—i.e., they are right and useful if they enhance Christian love; they are dangerous and wrong if they hinder it. Even if this is regarded as a general ethical principle, the most antinomian situationalist could give his assent. As is the case with most other principles, by itself it does not deal with a lot of problems. What constitutes hindrance or enhancement, and how does one make such decisions? These obviously are the immediate and attendant issues, to be dealt with in the following chapter. But for now I wish to assert the valid and necessary place for noble ideals within a Christian ethical system. They belong on the same level and can best be handled in the same way as natural law principles.

Flexibility

Among the other ethical ingredients necessary for the synthesis is flexibility. While natural law and ideals are essentially ingredients of substance and content, flexibility is more obviously an attitude and a method. We have already noted flexibility as a characteristic of situational ethics, and one that is desirable. Rome, too, has had its share of flexibility, so it is present in both traditions. Since it is, in practice, essentially a means, a tool, it can easily be misused. So the emphasis I wish to put here is on flexibility as an attitude. One can have a series of rigid moral rules yet be fairly flexible in their application. In fact, if there are enough rules in a big system, one can always seek out some other rule to bend or break the obvious one that stands in the way! This can be done for good or ill, which brings us back to the old problem of right use, and what determines the right use of a tool, means, or attitude. I believe that, ultimately, the determination of flexibility must be derived from the one and only absolute—God's love in Christ. That must determine how rigid or loose I will be in applying this or that principle, rule, or rubric. Surely this is what Jesus meant when he talked about the spirit vs. the letter of the law.

Even so, the dangers of extremes are apparent. We have repeatedly warned Rome of a too-easy identification of reason— especially ecclesiastical reason—with God's reason. So, also, must we warn Protestants about the too-easy identification of our motive of love with God's love. If inflexibility leads to unjust moralism, unrestrained and unchecked flexibility can lead to anarchy and self-righteousness. Flexibility we must have, but it must be under the aegis of love, guided by principles and ethics, and checked by fellow Christians who constitute the church.

Secular Knowledge

Finally, secular knowledge seems to be an obvious part of anybody's ethical system, secular or sacred. Yet it is painfully true that many religious persons and institutions ignore relevant factual knowledge. Some even assume that good motives and high ideals are enough. Thus, people have written their congressmen telling them "to vote for honesty." Churches have passed many resolutions calling for peace and justice, using noble slogans and clichés—all quite futile. But lack of facts may lead not to futility but to real injustice. For example, one can adopt the attitude that "in foreign policy, the President knows best; he has all the sources of information and expert advice, so we must support him and his policy." [14] But such an attitude enables one to avoid the homework of getting at the truth. Even worse, it endorses a policy uncritically. And if the policy is more evil than good, then one has contributed to the extension of evil. Some people and some churches have stood guilty of precisely this posture in Nazi Germany, Communist Russia, and—if one regards the Vietnam war as immoral—in the United States.

In less awesome and dramatic issues, the point remains the same. How can a Christian act morally and responsibly on a problem if he does not have adequate information about the situation and the nature of the problem? A good heart and noble intentions will not tell him which tax bill is fair, which poverty bill is the most adequate, or which person is most qualified for a job. He must do his homework and learn about the situation from many sources. Given our past failures in fact-gathering, and given the difficulty of obtaining adequate information, the need for knowledge in ethical decision and moral action is gigantic.

As with our theological conclusions, so now regarding our

ethical conclusions: I believe both traditions can agree on the inclusion of the ethical ingredients outlined in this chapter. There may be differences of emphasis and description, but surely there can be agreement on the primacy of Christian love, the need for natural, rational principles, noble ideals, adequate knowledge, and flexible application. These are surely the ethical bases of any meaningful synthesis.

Thus far, however, we have covered the relatively easy part, in spite of some very basic problems. Most of the really difficult issues will surface as I now try to show a better way of using Christian ethics. Most everyone can agree on the nobility and desirability of ethics (as of ideals), but it is in application and action that the difficult issues appear. The test of a theory or a model is its use in practical, everyday action. So it is my duty to indicate as carefully as I am able in the remainder of the book how this theoretical alliance or synthesis can be used to achieve a more effective way of Christian ethical behavior.

Chapter
VI

A BETTER WAY OF USING CHRISTIAN ETHICS

Thus far I have outlined the nature of the theological and ethical ingredients of the proposed alliance or synthesis between love and natural law. I have noted possible problems, suggested preliminary agreements, and postponed until now a fuller discussion of the critical difficulties involved. It is my contention that the most creative opportunities as well as the most serious dangers can best be seen as we try to deal with examples in several areas of personal and social problems. First, however, let us describe the priority of values in our ethical structure.

The Priority of Values

1. *Love.* For the Christian, the one and only absolute is God's love as revealed in the special revelation in Christ. While we shall define the nature of this love later, it will suffice now to emphasize the point that this kind of love is our absolute yardstick, our measurement for moral judgments, the source of love power; it is, for us, our Ultimate Reality.

2. *General Ethical Principles.* Under this broad heading, I would suggest two categories: personal inner attitudes and external social actions. Personal inner attitudes include such "be-attitudes" as honesty, prudence, fortitude, integrity (mean-

ing a whole inner quality of life), inner freedom, and personal ideals. External social actions include such natural rational principles as justice, temperance, kindness, the need for the state and the family, order, liberty, equality, and the common good. This list of internal and external principles and ideals obviously could be expanded, but my purpose is only to give a sample. In fact and in practice, the proposed structure would be filled with many noble ideals from all races and all sources, Christian, non-Christian, Oriental, Occidental. One need not categorize them as I have done. There are some who might prefer to list the ethical ingredients as principles under the classifications "prescriptive" and "illuminative," or "advisory" and "regulative," or other such groupings. The only point I would make concerns the *place* assigned to general ethical principles, virtues, and ideals. The proper place is *under* the authority of love. This means that *none* of the principles is absolute, only love is. At the same time, it also means that we are not establishing a priority of principles and ethical values. They are all equal in the formal structure; they all belong in the household. Later, when applied to a specific moral problem, priority will be established. But I see no need to establish a hierarchy of formal values. History suggests that any such attempt is culturally corrupted and almost infinitely varied. The relativity of application seems to me to preclude any rigid assignment of priorities, particularly if we have our one and only absolute. So what happens in effect is that all great virtues and ethical principles, natural law, and other innumerable ideals are given penultimate status in the household of faith. So, if love is first, principles and ideals are second.

3. *Style of Life (Ethos).* The third priority is the ethos or life-style of the ethical home. In contemporary terms, it is sometimes called the "ambience." Obviously, there could be many types of styles. But whatever the form, I should want to have at least the following basic elements present: openness of attitude, sensitivity of spirit, humor (the necessity of

not taking oneself too seriously), trust in self and in the household, and the desire to experiment with new things in new ways. Yet one does not wish to fill out a life-style in detail, for fear of making it too rigid. Thus, this ethos or ambience sounds vague and nebulous—and it is. Perhaps the focus can be made sharper if a contrast is drawn, even if it is an extreme one. Picture the worst kind of moral prude, a person who lacks self-confidence and seeks to avoid all possible guilt. Therefore he wants specific, rigid rules guaranteed by external authority. Such a person will do the obvious good and avoid obvious evil. When faced with complex situations, he will ignore the subtleties and extract a simple solution. If the solution fails, he will make sure that it was not *he* who failed, but "they"! He is the very model of the "uptight" person: humorless, loveless, severe, rigid, and self-righteous. Everyone can agree that this style of life is to be abhorred. This is the ethos we do not want.

On the other hand, this caricature does not establish the desirability of its opposite. We are not idolizing the carefree, iconoclastic, amoral, swinging extrovert. There are too many valid and healthy personality types to choose only one as an ideal. So we will continue to have people of great integrity and moral maturity, yet some will be of the rough-diamond type, others meek and mild appearing, some flashily aggressive, others complex and baffling. Regardless of the personality, all we want are some of the "be-attitudes" listed in our ethos. For example, the *way* in which one argues, makes observations, or offers criticism greatly enhances or hinders the facing of the issue at hand. If one blurts out bluntly and dogmatically, You're wrong on that; how could you be so immoral?—obviously the victim's defenses will rise and he will reject the declaration even if it is true. By contrast, one might make the same point and have a better reception if he says: I'm not sure we're altogether right on that decision; maybe we overlooked part of the problem; would you reconsider reviewing the issues before we go any farther? If these words seem too soft, others can be used. Whatever the words, the subtle but essential thing is "attitude" or atmosphere expressed in the light touch, maybe a smile, the right tone of voice—not harsh and condemnatory—but preferably one of sincere concern and sensitivity to the other person. This is what I mean by style or ethos.

4. *Knowledge*. I would place fourth the need for relevant knowledge of situations. Since we have stressed this point before, it is not necessary to discuss it again. Let us just make sure we have a place for it.

5. *Application*. Finally, the process of using the basic elements of the ethical alliance completes our structure. In summary form, then, our ethics consist of: Love—Principles (Ideals)—Ethos—Knowledge—Action. Now let us see how we can put them to work.

Personal Ethics

By personal ethics I mean those moral decisions which an individual makes about himself or about interpersonal relationships. The most obvious and common personal ethical problem is sex.

Since others have written on "the theology of sex," it is not necessary for me to do so. Two major points, however, need highlighting: First, the Biblical, Christian faith regards sex as essentially good. Thus, the major ethical question is the use or misuse of sex. Secondly, the Christian view of the basic unity of the self requires emphasis in the light of many contemporary cultural viewpoints that regard sex as a separate and autonomous phenomenon.

As one who has counseled and taught college students for over twenty-five years, I can testify to the vast number who have thought they could solve their "sex problem" by some sex action. Further, many also felt that sex was *the* answer to many other problems: loneliness, anxiety, boredom, egoism, manliness. Amateur interpreters of Freud have contributed to the notion that sex is *the* cause of personality problems and is therefore *the* cure. The recent increase in "skin flicks," pornography, and sexual violence add to the cultural cliché that what is real and significant is sex.

It is essential, therefore, to reaffirm both the Christian and the scientific view that while sex is *a* basic part of human nature, it is heavily influenced by the rest of the personality and vice versa. The interaction of all parts of the self seems obvious and true enough, yet it has to be emphasized again and again.

Premarital Sex

Let us now turn to a specific moral problem in order to begin to demonstrate *how* our ethical system might function. One of the most common moral problems of college students today is the question of premarital sex. This question is usually narrowed down to the issue of whether premarital sexual intercourse is moral or not. But a larger context is the proper place to begin the ethical analysis. First, if we are true to our "system," we begin with Christian love. Translated into broader and more contemporary terms the question is: What is the most loving thing to do in the sexual situation? This suggests our primary guide and goal. Secondly, we ask: Are there any natural law principles that can be used as helpful guides for conduct? The answer is that there are many, such as the principles of maturity, self-control, virginity, integrity, and the right use of sex.

Thirdly, the ethos of our life-style will seek openness and honesty in interpersonal relationships; gaiety, humor, and fun, as well as significance and meaning. Fourthly, the facts of the situation tell us that perhaps the biggest part of the problem is egoism. By egoism we mean the deep and powerful drive that tends to make us focus everything on our own private selves. It is that drive which tempts me to think that I am the center of everything; not that I am godlike, though that appears occasionally in extreme cases. For most of us, however, egoism is the deep attitude which says: "I am my first and most basic concern"; "I'm looking out for number one"; "What's in it for me?" This is a normal and natural human tendency, and it is especially powerful and dominant during adolescence.

The most important part of the problem at hand, therefore, is the relationship between egoism and sex. When egoism is our dominant drive, it will use sex as a vehicle for its own satisfactions, aggressions, and desires. This fact, in turn, results in the misuse of persons. Others are used as means to serve private needs and desires; people are manipulated. This may be true even if there is mutual consent. Personal relationships are not made moral because two people agree to torture each other or to misuse each other.

So the first major part of our problem is to find out how much egoism and adolescence there is in the specific situation at hand. For our example, let us assume we are dealing with a sixteen-year-old male. It is a fair assumption, I think, to assert that the amount of egoism dominant in his behavior is somewhere around 75 percent. In his relationship with girls, then, most of his motivation will be to use them for his own wants. Of course, not all his wants and needs are morally evil; few are. He has curiosity, wonder, awe, fear, passions, all kinds of human feelings and emotions. The point is that his dominant drive behind all these personality factors is egoistic satisfaction. Again, not all the "satisfactions" are bad, but the *method* he uses may be bad. Egoism wants instant response and will use almost anyone or anything to achieve it.

Now a value interpretation is introduced. Love calls for caring about persons, for treating them as free, unique individuals, as ends. From love's viewpoint, egoism is wrong because it tends to deny or prevent love. In this case, one is misusing persons, treating them as means; one is not interested in their well-being, only his own. So our primary ethical judgment is that egoism is wrong because it is unlovely.

Next, we have to consider the 25 percent of non-egoism in our sixteen-year-old. Let us assume that this 25 percent consists of healthy desires for friendship, growth, knowledge, self-confidence, "ego-identity," fun, excitement, and adventure. This part of his self will seek to like and be liked by both sexes, to find out about "life" and problems, about possible vocations. One would expect, therefore, that in his relationship with girls he will want genuinely to know *a* girl, if not several, to really begin to appreciate girls for their own sakes. When he does, dating, hand-holding, and soon kissing and necking will occur. This is premarital sex. When this stage of "friendship" has been reached, then the more specific question is asked: How far should one go? But our prior reply will be to provide a general framework under which a more specific answer might be given. The general framework we have tried to describe in this typical example of the sixteen-year-old. Our conclusion of his adolescence-maturity ratio, or his egoism-caring ratio (expressed in percentages) is about 75–25. What this means, ethically, is that 25 percent of his relationship is morally acceptable. His beginning friendship, hand-holding, and kissing *are* all expressions of friendly caring. On the other hand, 75 percent of his actions will be egoistic, and therefore he should *not* use sex as a servant of his adolescence. Specifically, then, we would caution him not to engage in prolonged necking and petting, and would say a firm No to sexual intercourse.

Naturally, some wag at this point would raise the question: Why not 25 percent of him for intercourse? The reply is that since sexual intercourse is one of the most intimate and profound actions, it should be reserved for the deepest expressions of love. Twenty-five percent is not rich enough in our process.

From what has been said so far, one can see the ideal model we are trying to build. The general principle is that sex should be used as a vehicle for, and an expression of, caring love, not adolescent egoism. The amount of sex should be determined by the amount of mature love. Because the mixture is always ambiguous no detailed rules on necking vs. petting can be made. The nearest effective principle, in our judgment, would be determined by the approximate amount of maturity vs. adolescence, love vs. egoism, that is present. That is to say, if a boy spends most of his time trying to figure out how he can maneuver a date into bed, then this is a pretty reliable sign that egoism, not love, is in charge. By contrast, if a man sees the girl for her wider self, plans a diverse weekend or date, taking into account her needs and interests, including the sexual, it would appear that a fair amount of mature caring is present.

So to the question, How far to go? I would offer no specific rules, but I would relate sexual activity as well as all other relationships to the ratio of egoism and love. In my ideal model, I would draw the line at sexual intercourse. I would argue that, ideally, these actions are best experienced in mature love and should be reserved for the marriage adventure. At the same time, I would not regard this ideal as an absolute. One can think of a number of valid exceptions. For example, if someone has a neurotic hang-up about sex and intercourse, perhaps accompanied by fantasy illusions about a cure-all ecstasy, or some awesome fear of it, then it is quite conceivable that a psychiatrist would urge the patient to go out and experience and "get it (the fantasy or fear) over with." My only comment in such instances is to add the caution: But don't let the amateur use reasons like this to sanctify sleeping around. Or to use another example: Two mature medical students in their middle twenties have wandered into a developing friendship. Real caring occurs, thus making it difficult to see why intercourse in their case is not an experience of their caring.

Let us now review what we have been discussing. Our absolute is love, our general ideal and model is that sex is to be used as an expression of love. Therefore to the adolescent and the egoist—regardless of physical age—I say: Don't use sex for a private ego trip. As with all new and basic things, you must learn about it, practice it gently, until you can begin to understand it, master it, control it. But most important, it is essential that you do not regard "*it*" as something separate. What needs to be worked on is not sex, but your egoism, your adolescence, your overall maturity, and your capacity to love. *That* is what will largely determine your capacity to master sex and receive maximum satisfaction.

Similarly, I have proposed a definite rule about no intercourse before marriage. Yet it is not an absolute rule, and my model recognizes exceptions. More than that, it is equally necessary to recognize failures, mistakes, "slips" among growing adolescents. As with any other mistake, failure, or sin, the procedure is not to cast the one who commits it into outer darkness. On the other hand, we do not celebrate the mistake as a great act of freedom, a virile "playboy conquest," or the arrival at manhood. From our point of view, depending on the motives and the situation, it may not have been some foul sin, but it is less than the achievable best. And what we are most interested in is not "condemnation" but progress toward the best. Therefore, let us call it a "mistake" and let us seek to improve the growth in love.

To sharpen this argument, let us give another example of the kind of moral analysis and application used in our approach. We have said that our ideal model includes chastity before marriage—for the vast majority of growing adolescents. We have noted exceptions and noted also the need to make clear judgments about "mistakes"—i.e., violations of the model. Some might prefer a stronger label than "mistake" for an act of premarital intercourse. My response is to say that it would depend on how much real love was violated and the person misused, on the amount of manipulative egoism present, and not just on the act itself. Thus, one could imagine a couple intending to "play it straight," but, in the "situation" of special romance and tenderness one night, they "slipped." I would not regard this as a severe violation, a big immoral act; I would classify it only as an understandable mistake of no serious consequence. By contrast, if some egoistic playboy got his date drunk or "high," enticed her up to his room and necked and petted and pawed her, and for some reason did not engage in intercourse (perhaps she or he "passed out"), I would regard those actions as far more serious than those of the couple who "slipped." The important point is that I consider this a greater violation, and the reason is obvious. One was clearly a violation of love, a serious misuse of a person; the other was not a violation of love but only a step short of self-mastery, a small halt on the road to an ideal.

By contrast, if one makes chastity into a near-absolute rule, then its violation assumes a high priority of condemnation. Hence in the two examples above, the couple would be severely judged; the playboy less so, for he broke no specific law, only an apparently vague category of egoism vs. love, use vs. misuse. Yet, as we all know, the playboy is far more immoral than the couple. Historically and practically, however, one can also see why clear rules are so attractive. How easy it is for parents, teachers, and ecclesiastical authorities to administer rules and codes; how "vague and indefinite" it is to administer general concepts such as maturity, egoism, self-mastery and noncompulsive behavior. Faced with complexity and ambiguity, most of us want a clear-cut, simple answer. And, most of the time, the church has obliged us. When it has been greatly successful, we then find ourselves enslaved: rules become tyrants, persons are sacrificed to principles, and tradition overcomes the Spirit. Then an explosion occurs; the pendulum swings to the other extreme. "Freedom from" is all, "doing my own thing" is king, and "live and let live" is the easy social ethic. What this book advocates is a classic middle ground between the extremes. Whether this can be done remains to be seen.

In the discussion of premarital sex, most of the focus so far has centered around the most common problem, namely, that of sexual intercourse. Because it is usually the first question, we have tried to respond to it. At the same time, I want to reemphasize that, in my judgment, the specific act is *not* the central problem of premarital sex. While I offer a general principle of virginity before marriage, the higher ideal is a general model of maturity and love. And it is this more basic area which needs to be developed.

Perhaps a short, dogmatic sentence will provide the clue to what I am trying to describe, i.e.: "The problem of sex is not a sexual problem." This concept is *a* way of stating the need to see sex in its relationship to total self and especially to the process of mature love. I believe the best way to determine which principles and ideals should be applied to problems of premarital sex is to outline "the big picture" of mature and responsible love. Most people would agree on the basic ingredients. It is easy to draw ideal models. But the heart of the problem is how to apply the ideal to unideal people and unideal situations. One can describe the difficulty in inductive and deductive terms: e.g., how does one progress from the realistic mix toward the more noble, right ideal? and how does one apply the ideal to the real? In both cases, it is the process and principle of selection of helpful guides that constitutes the real use of ethics, casuistry, and moral action.

So let us now consider another common problem, that of parental "advice" to an average teen-ager about "premarital sexual behavior," not just sexual intercourse. Consistent with our earlier dogma that the problem of sex is not sex, we begin by affirming that indeed the primary problem is really interpersonal relations, the concept of the self, egoism, maturity, and love. This means that through a variety of ways, parents and children have to establish communication. Then the substance of the "conversations" will have to include mutual education about how adolescent egoism displays itself: the direct and indirect symptoms of it in attitudes and actions, the mercurial change of moods. At the same time, awareness of what constitutes early signs of maturity would be included; tentative distinctions between adolescent and mature love must be

noted. Deeper than these gradual discoveries is the atmosphere of the relationship, e.g., the respect and caring concern for each other, the firmness but fairness in family responsibilities. And finally, what ethical principles and moral
rules are involved? What we have described so far is the
primary need for the presence of love, and the need for
knowing "the facts" of adolescent egoism and mature love,
but now we must try to see where the rules come in! There
are many helpful ethical principles such as: "Thou shalt not
abuse people nor play games with people's feelings." Or if one
wants something more specific: "Thou shalt not mix alcohol,
drugs, and cars." Other rules have to do with how late one
can stay out, or the relationship between weekday night dates
and school homework. The key issue is not the specific or
general rule, but *how* the rule is administered. If the specific
rule becomes an absolute, the whole relationship will begin
to deteriorate. On the other hand, if the customs or rules are
ignored, or if the general principles are overlooked, the moral
process and interpersonal relationship will also decline. The
"right" application of moral guides is done in an atmosphere
of love, trust, and firmness. Thus, if there has been a violation
of the return-at-midnight rule, the proper approach is to find
out why it was not observed. And to do so without subtle
inferences of condemnation such as: "Did you get stoned?"
The query is purely factual with the ethos of caring. Then,
if and when the facts are disclosed, *mutual* judgment should
lead to an acceptable solution. The result sought for is not
punishment but helpful ways to develop more responsibility.
And it may be that after a while, or shortly, a 1 A.M. curfew
is decided upon as a better rule.

One can see that this is only a sketchy outline of an almost
universal family problem. There are all kinds of variations,
real and potential. The two key points I wish to stress are:
(1) the basic atmosphere of love and (2) the right use of
principles and rules. Everybody can agree on the desirability
of the first. It is the second point which is controversial. To

the extreme situationalist, I would emphasize that there should be present in the family, general ethical principles, definite moral guides, and specific family rules. To the legalist or extreme moral formalist, I would emphasize that *the* important thing is not the preservation of principles or rules at all costs, but the growth of mature love in the family. To all concerned, then, we are asserting the "middle" role, the helpful, guiding role of ethics and morals. The principle of selection is Christian love and consideration of the persons involved. By that yardstick we shall determine which principle should be emphasized, which rule changed, which rule held firm.

If we now apply this "model" to adolescent sexual behavior, our example might be that of a family where at least 51 percent love abounds in the household. In a variety of ways, this family learns about the relationship of egoism to love. The various means include family arguments, lost tempers, impulsive actions, selfish claims, plus a desire to get along with each other, to share, and to help. These are the daily examples of the blend of egoism and love. Through this process, by experience, by design, and by demonstrative action, persons learn what is meant by loving concern, or its opposite—misuse of others. Father may be concerned about his family, but if his son sees the curt, arrogant way the father treats the gas station attendant, or hears his muttering about "those damn Jews," "niggers," "hippies," "honkies," or whatever, then the son will have learned something about adult sin and the mixture of love and egoism in the father. By contrast, caring, sensitive relations with "all sorts and conditions" of people in daily life is worth a thousand family "discussions."

Our ambience in the family is something like that described above. Now let us see where and how ethics can be used. A mother's advice to the daughter can certainly include "what every woman knows," but can also include discussion of how adolescent boys tend to use girls for their private growing-up problems, and vice versa. More specifically, a spelling out—

especially after an unhappy date—of what it means to play jealousy games, to use big "buildup lines," to dangle or seduce. The emphasis here will be on use and misuse of people, inner freedom, ego identity, love of self—valid and invalid. And it is within these contexts of these basic problems that one can more clearly define the general ethical principles of misuse of self or sex on other persons. It is within these areas that more specific rules and morals will be of practical use.

Thus, a mother can put her O.K. on a lot of small talk, coquetting, using "lines" for a while in the banter stage, but call a halt on "games" when she sees that deeper feelings or hopes are aroused. Then it is time to be honest, to say and to do what you feel is right about the relationship. And it is within such contexts that one sets up an ethics of sex—namely, first, that one must learn to master and control his own sexual desires and needs, and secondly, that sex is best used and most satisfying when it is an expression of love. From this it follows that one should not simply give in to every momentary impulse of the sex drive when it appears; to do so is to lose self-mastery. Nor should one kiss and neck with anybody on any date. That is to degrade the self, increasing egoism as well as indulging the egoism of the partner, consenting or not. Here then are some general but definite ethical principles about sex. I would argue that, if explained and administered with clarity, they are generally true, right, and very helpful to the child.

The more difficult set of problems arises not with the "loose woman" or the "playboy," but with the nice, average boy and girl who are going steady, who are real, honest friends, if not already in love in a "wildly adolescent" way. What rules apply in this situation? The general applicable principles will still center around the mixture of egoism and adolescence. Parents tend to regard their sons and daughters as more adolescent, and sons and daughters think themselves more mature, than they really are. Even so, the awareness of the mix is essential, even if the exact amount cannot be determined or agreed upon. Next, awareness of the amount of compulsion for sex is needed. Is there a blend of sexual and nonsexual activity on a date? What, in general, is the ratio? How much pressure is there to go the whole way, and if so, why? Then awareness of the relation of alcohol and drugs is essential. Are they being used as a means to seduce one or both? Is someone becoming dependent upon chemistry for a good time, or to feel aggressive, or to gain confidence, or to become more sexy? If these symptoms are discernible, one can lay down some rules: if one is dependent on pot for sex or security, one is in trouble. It is immoral to use chemistry to break down someone's will. It is immoral to use drugs to run away from a problem which could be solved with normal effort. Prolonged necking all the time on every date is immoral, not because it's "sexual," but because it is damaging to the freedom of the self and one's control over the self, and it is prolonging adolescent egoism.

From these moral guides, one can go on to make family rules about times for getting home, about no overnights spent together, or about how to handle this and that type of situation on a date. Changing these rules and customs when the child "grows up" and goes away to college is part of the problem of freedom and maturity. When the child leaves home, physically, to go to school, or to work, or to "road trip," parental control is ended in any regular or influential way. The child is now on his own, for good or ill. His previous family values and attitudes should be part of himself, but outwardly they will probably be in eclipse. This is why I have concentrated at length on the adolescent period, for this marks the final stage of parental daily communication and the beginning of freedom from the rules for the child. This is why I am trying to emphasize the presence of ethical principles and rules for the sexual behavior of the adolescent. At the same time, I am also trying to emphasize that though the rules are there, they are dependent upon self-mastery, identity, caring love, and maturity. It is often assumed that the adolescent will "go too far," break both the rules and the principles.

The essential response to violations should not be punishment, assertion of parental ego or authority. Rather, the response seeks knowledge by the child of the standards, ideals, and rules; it fosters his growing awareness of their guiding relevance as well as of his mixture of approaching growth and the likelihood of common "slips" or outright ego failures; lastly it seeks his knowledge that the whole purpose of the ethics and the parental guidance is precisely loving, just concern for him. In sum, rigid punishment for violations of rigid rules will enslave a child; no rules and no application tell the child that the parent doesn't care. The ambience of love makes possible the flexible use of principles and rules.

Extramarital Sex

The Christian model of marriage has always assumed a lifelong love commitment, a monogamous marriage, and therefore sexual fidelity to each partner. Specifically, Christian ethics does not approve of extramarital intercourse. This writer agrees with the model and the ethical principle. But as is easily guessed by now, I would not regard either the model or the principle as absolutes. Thus, for example, I believe in the ethical duty of divorce under certain circumstances. When love is dead and no children are involved, I see no real purpose served by the couple living together either in indifference or hostility. Divorce seems to me to be the right action. Assuming that some learning from the unhappiness has occurred and that normal love–egoism ratios are present, I believe that both people should be able to seek love and marriage again with someone else.

Similarly with sex in marriage. I believe that sex is most creatively expressed, controlled, and directed within the marriage situation. Because it is an expression of profound love, its satisfactions are the deepest. Real ecstasy on all levels occurs in this type of deep, loving relationship: this is the greatest. Are there, then, to be no possible exceptions? Deane

Ferm gives an example of a married man who has some inner problems, and suggests that therapy might require or advise him to sleep with somebody else occasionally.[15] Whatever the problem of the man might be, it is difficult for me to see how one can turn this therapy into an ethical principle about sex or a moral rule of suggested behavior. The only relevant moral principle involved is to follow the advice of medical science, assuming it is scientific, and assuming it does not violate an equally intense personal ethical principle. Ferm's exception may be psychiatrically valid, but that is quite different from making such therapy into a sexual or moral rule. I would therefore want to emphasize that the ethical norm is fidelity, and that while therapy may be needed, such actions as necessitate therapy are signs of trouble, problems, and weaknesses. They are not to be made into excuses for abandoning the norm or for pretending that there is no qualitative or moral difference between fidelity and therapy, or between fidelity and promiscuity. Here again, Rome has tended to absolutize the norm and be harsh on the violator, while Geneva has tended to be easier with the practitioner, but has sold out to contemporary moral anarchy (usually in the name of "love" or "freedom" or "relevance" or "reality"). By contrast, I want to emphasize that one of the functions of Christian ethics is to make clear its principles, and one of the functions of casuistry and practical moral action is to make clear the moral mixture in behavior, especially the exceptions. To put it bluntly and specifically, if a man is really deeply in love with his wife—if there is a mature and profound and exciting relationship on all levels—then why does he want to sleep with somebody else? I very much doubt whether he can claim it is essential for his therapy, or that it will increase his sense of diversity and therefore make him appreciate his wife the more. I would argue that these are "phony" rationalizations. What is more likely, it seems to me, is that under the pressure of a long business trip beset with many delicate problems, and having one too many drinks with a company secretary, a man might end up in bed with the woman. This is perhaps understandable, but even so let us call the event by its proper name: It is *not* "the best moral action under the circumstances"; it *is* a betrayal of fidelity to his wife; it *is* a common human weakness. He need not fry in hell; it is not his most serious sin; it need not ruin his marriage. Yet the act was a lapse (not morally great) and needs attention, or it will lead to future trouble through repetition.

From this example one can see the emphasis I am trying to make: it is essential to define and label one's principles, rules, and actions in order to apply them as accurately as possible to specific deeds. And, as in the case above, several labels or descriptive rules may apply. But the other essential emphasis must be on how one treats both the deed and the doer. And here we are not searching around to see if we can find the most serious violation in order to make the condemnation more clear and incisive. On the contrary, we are primarily interested in the improvement (i.e., the redemption) of the person. So what is called for are these accurate labelings, humanely applied. This avoids sloppy permissiveness on the one hand and self-righteous condemnation on the other hand. In sum, then, I believe Christian ethics to be clearly against extramarital sex, but when violations do occur they are to be treated like the breaking of any other ethical principle or moral rule. Because close and intimate love is involved, as well as perhaps a family, a violation of this kind of love is much more serious than telling a lie, for instance, or stealing an apple. The priority of seriousness is determined by how much love is involved.

Before concluding this discussion of sex, I must add that one of the basic assumptions behind my descriptions of premarital sex is the presence of the best goal of mature married love. That is what most people want. The ethical principles of self-mastery, maturity, self-giving, and reduction of egoism are all ingredients that can lead to a wonderful marriage. If one wants to attain a fabulous life together, the process I have outlined is the best way to obtain it. It needs to be noted, however, that not all people want to get married, and a lot of people are willing to settle for mediocrity either by ignorance of anything better, or by choice. (There are even some who do not think "the best" is that good or worth the cost.) Since this is the situation for many people, what then is the Christian position on sex for them?

For those who wish to remain single in life, the ethical principles are the same, namely, the kind and amount of sexual activity should be determined by the ratio of egoism and love operative in the person, the motives, and the situation. Thus, if a single person engages frequently and compulsively in sex, using it as an escape from boredom and problems, a means of ego aggression, or whatever, we would say this is a misuse of sex, of the self, and of love, and therefore immoral. On the other hand, if a meaningful friendship, a caring concern between two consenting adults occurs, sex between them may be a valid expression of their love and friendship. Their one additional responsibility to be assumed is the outside possibility of a child. Granted that the chance is very slim (given modern contraceptives), nevertheless if an offspring occurs, it is their responsibility, rather than that of their relations or of public agencies. This possibility should be present in the decision before the action occurs. The difficulty here, of course, is that precisely because the chance is so unlikely, the responsibility factor is just as likely never to be present. The assumption is: "It only happens to other people." For this reason it needs to be pointed out as a danger spot in such a situation. Even so, the Christian view of sexuality and its relation to egoism, love, and friendship—caring concern—does not preclude sexuality outside of or prior to marriage. The mature, married, profound love is the highest ideal. A nonmarried loving friendship is not as lofty or as profound a relationship, but it is nonetheless moral or ethical. And the analytical yardstick is still the same: caring love, the need to curb exploitation and egoism—and other such principles.

As for those who live on the mediocrity level, our ethical principles are the same. For a variety of reasons, and not all by choice, many people are in a nonfamily situation, beset by physical poverty and a mediocre culture, i.e., as far as healthy interpersonal relations go. The ideal or near-ideal is not a real possibility for them. Even mere survival in the ghetto is an achievement. For many, the desperate pleasure choice is only between shooting heroin or engaging in sex. All else is hell. On a different level, many a middle-class home has only a mediocre quality of life, or worse. There is little likelihood of children knowing about or being able to achieve the ideal. In such situations, what is the realistic thing to do?

Again, my response would be to aim for the ideal and abide by the same ethical principles. But again it is the *how* of their application to these "realistic situations" that needs to be answered. It seems to me that one begins with a caring concern to find out the specific situation and how much self-knowledge, discovery, and improvement is possible. Most likely a very high level is not at all possible. Therefore one tries to encourage persons to achieve the best that they can within their situation. In terms of specific deeds, this means, sexually, for example, that there will be a lot of "sleeping around," egoistic and exploitive sexuality—a lot of it mutual, some not. Our ethical analysis and moral judgment will not call such behavior good; it is a violation of love, it is *bad* (there, we said it plainly!). We have now judged the deed. But how shall we treat the doers of the deed? The Biblical answer is equally clear: we shall not condemn them, nor shall we make them into sidewalk saints. If, in their situation, they have reduced their egoism from 90 percent to 75 percent, great should be our rejoicing. If in desperate poverty or appalling blandness of mediocrity a person improves a little, let him shame us for not doing likewise in our more favorable circumstances. You will note that we have not given up or compromised ethical principles: I have called a spade a spade; but I have also tried to administer morals with love. The ancient Christian prayer sums it up best: "O God, give us an abiding hatred of the wrong we oppose, and a generous forgiveness to the doer of it."

Secondly, we stated at the outset that the Christian view of marriage has been that of the ideal lifelong monogamous partnership, and that this model has heavily influenced our application of ethical principles to sexuality. I believe it is important to note that as high an ideal as this model may be, it is not the only possible one. We have already stated in our poverty illustration that such a model is probably an impossible ideal, and high as our ideal may be, it is still not our absolute. These two facts suggest the possibility of other possible ideals, other types of family life.

As culture changes, new forms of life-style may develop. The point is that *how* a man and wife shall cleave to each other may involve different styles of life. There is nothing absolute or uniquely sacred about the American suburbia model. Nor am I impressed with the Continental custom of marrying a hausfrau and maintaining mistresses. Concubinage and harems seem to me to be based primarily on male egoism and dominance. Nevertheless, present and past styles do not automatically exclude the possibility of a new and valid marriage style. The ingredients of progressive and profound love and mutual sharing "for richer for poorer, in sickness and in health" are still the Christian basis of the family. And if children are involved, it is less than responsible to farm them out to nurseries and nannies from the crib on up. Even so, I believe we should be open to new ways in which the "old love" can be realized. For example, faced with the impersonality of city apartment life and the bland sameness of many Levittown-type suburban homes, it may be that small groups of five or ten families will form a semi-commune or develop a new style of "togetherness." But again, let it be emphasized: the basic essentials of Christian love and fidelity—the achievable and the highest ideal—must be the standard and the goal. The architecture of the house may vary; the substance and quality of life to be sought for will not.

Birth Control and Euthanasia

I have chosen these two moral problems because they illustrate most sharply the differences in basic ethical principles, if not in theology, between Rome and Geneva. If the differences can be clearly delineated, perhaps the possibilities for accommodation and rapprochement can also be indicated.

Birth Control. According to Roman Catholic ethics, the church is *not* against birth control; it is against artificial contraceptives. Official writings endorse "the rhythm method." It would seem, then, that Rome has introduced a concept of natural function as the primary criterion. By contrast, it is implied that man-made contraceptives are both antinatural and interfering with natural process. One can find assertions in some Catholic writings that the primary, and perhaps the essential, function of sexual intercourse is the procreation of children. In other Catholic writings one can also find admissions that intercourse can also be a valid expression of love without necessarily having the intent of procreation. However, the basic argument seems to be that the primary natural purpose of sexual intercourse is to have children. On the other hand, the church recognizes that this concept is *not* always the highest principle. If the health of the mother is endangered, or if a large family is already living in poverty, birth control by rhythm should be exercised. It is therefore difficult to see why the concept of something "artificial" should suddenly be introduced. It is clear that the sex act is not always the guiding or regulative consideration; health, economic poverty, and—recently—psychological well-being have been given priority over the "natural sex act of procreation." Since Rome agrees on the validity of using medicine and surgery for human health and welfare, although they often interfere or alter "natural functions" and processes, why should it label immoral the use of something "artificial" to effect the same ends?

In all candor, I think it must be said that most of the defenses by Roman Catholics of their position do *not* deal with this "artificial" problem. Most arguments dredge up the possible abuses that could occur, the misuse that is likely, and future projections of decline in population and general morals "if everybody can just buy the pill over the counter." These *are* legitimate issues. They need to be discussed and appropriate actions need to be proposed. But the prior and central issue is the theological-ethical doctrine of nature and artificiality.

As a Protestant, I am sometimes tempted to use *ad hominem* (or *ad ecclesiam*) accusations that Rome's real motive is to keep the Catholic population always growing! But let us not judge others' motives; let us rather deal with the formal stated positions. Even so, I must say that I can see no possibility of agreement on the proposition that contraceptives are artificial and therefore immoral. The need for control, efficiency, protection against misuse, exploring the cultural by-products of the pill, and many more issues, I feel, can be handled cooperatively by Rome and Geneva. Meanwhile, if Rome cannot change its position on artificiality, we shall at least temporarily have to agree to disagree.

Euthanasia. The classical ethical principles against killing and murder would hardly seem debatable. Although "mercy killing" has always been a challenging problem, the issue has increased in scope and intensity in contemporary life. Part of the reason is that with modern medicine life has been prolonged, and even in serious and terminal cases life can be prolonged artificially in some form for an indefinite time. Another reason for challenging the ancient prohibitions is the revival of emphasis on the love ethic. Let us look at the problem.

One of the basic ethical principles, derived from natural law, is: "Thou shalt not kill." Another ancient principle is:

"Man does not have the right to decide when to end his natural life; only God does." It should be obvious that violation of these two principles can lead to slaughter in war, and general chaos through the wanton taking of life. These natural law principles are sound and important. Yet, if we are consistent with our Christian absolute, *the* controlling criterion is Christian love. If there are to be exceptions to the two natural law principles, they must be defined in terms of "the loving thing to do." The reasons for exceptions, and the "situation" that allows them, must be made clear.

In cases of euthanasia, natural law and moral theology apply another useful and helpful principle, namely, "letting nature take its course"; specifically, "letting a person die." Thus, in a desperate terminal case in which a patient is really kept alive only by medicine or machine, when considerable suffering is involved, the moral choice is between "continuation of life by any means" vs. the loving concern for the quality of existence for the patient. Roman Catholic moralists, in such instances, support the decision to withdraw the medicine or machine and let the patient die naturally. This is *not* regarded as murder or killing because the doctor is simply "letting nature take its course." Further, his intent is not to kill, but to abide by natural process. Therefore, such action is regarded as morally good. The ethical principles are natural and good and the primary motive is love.

Protestant situational ethics could agree with this decision, even if it does not want to use the intermediary natural law principles. For example, many people often experience moods of depression due to a number of causes, internal and/or external. If the depression is severe, one may be tempted to commit suicide. Or if someone beloved is in great suffering, whether psychological or physical, one may be tempted to engage in a "mercy killing" or persuade his doctor to do so. It is important to have in a society some ethical principles that remind people of the morality of inner integrity and social responsibility.

In this example, the relevance of these principles is to suggest that life is at least partly a gift, that the self is of value, that we owe something to our friends and relatives. Therefore, it is immoral to take life just because we feel unhappy or are in pain, or because life seems aimless or useless. Those common reasons are understandable and evoke one's sympathy and care, but by themselves, they are not sufficient to break the ethical principles. Without these principles, it is very easy to slide into an individualistic anarchy where "doing your own thing" or "my private right" can be used to justify almost anything. Even more important, both the individual and society need some protection against their own weaknesses and abuses. Neither we nor doctors in general want members of the medical profession to feel free to "mercy-kill" without compunction or check. The ethical principles of prohibition against suicide and "mercy killing," while guaranteeing no such success, do provide some restraint for some people, remind all of us of the preciousness of life, and offer reliable truth to tide us over a difficult time. I am trying to argue two points at the same time: First, I believe that the ethical principles of saving life and of the preciousness of life are true and right in themselves. Secondly I am showing the positive effect of their practical application.

If we stopped at this point, it would seem that we have come out flatly against euthanasia. But the careful reader can predict otherwise! Valuable as ethical principles are, none of them are absolute. So we return to our prime standard of love. This criterion, along with other contending principles, may lead one to sanction "mercy killings" in some situations. For example, a mongoloid baby is born. It is a severe case; an operation would be required just in order to provide an outside chance of preserving life for one or two years at most. Without the operation, the mongoloid would "live" for perhaps six months. What is the loving thing to do? What other ethical principles are applicable here?

It seems to me the following selection of principles is in

order, and would reflect the loving (i.e., the right) thing to do: First, we have already started with the concern of love. Secondly, there is the principle of saving life. Thirdly, the facts of the situation have been outlined. Fourthly, the medical situation raises the question of the type and quality of life present in the mongoloid. Obviously, this is one of nature's "mistakes." There is no meaningful quality of life and consciousness, and there is no potential or future—only degeneration and death. Purely in terms of the baby itself, it is at least debatable whether any good or love is expressed by letting nature's "mistake" live and by spending the money, time, and skill of the doctors for an operation. But if one adds the further consideration of the parents, other factors must be weighed also: the suffering of the parents, the cost of either care or an operation, and the problem of who shall make the decision. Application of the principle of quality of life and potential for further life does not favor the mongoloid. Love for the parents in their anguish and in the possible economic squeeze they face needs to be balanced against a mistake of nature. The verdict seems to me to be clearly in favor of the parents.

A more difficult example is old age. A tour through a nursing home brings vividly to one's consciousness the need for an ethics of geriatrics. In earlier times, death by gradual decay was kept fairly private. Aunt Agatha was assigned a back room and cared for by the household. In many ways this was the best method for a difficult situation because it was personal and entailed family care. On the other hand, this was variable depending on the type of family and the type of degenerative illness. If the elderly person required professional care—physically or psychologically—public hospitalization was the usual answer. Since geriatrics is not the prime interest of most hospitals, this type of care was often minimal at best and scandalous at worst. Hence the origin of nursing homes, the reasons for which are many and varied. On the whole, medically at least, old-age care is better now than previously. This advance in medical care also partly increases the ethical problem because it results in prolongation of life.

Consequently we are now faced with some serious ethical and moral problems that properly come under the heading of euthanasia or "mercy killing." Here is a common example: Mrs. A is eighty-five years old, has lived a full life and been happily married. Her children are grown and on their own. She has arteriosclerosis in the form of harmless mental instability. She is fully conscious and rational at times, but then fades off into illusion, fantasy, and memory. She has all the beginnings of minor sufferings due to various degenerative failures. She has been in the nursing home for two years, is now hardly able to walk or to see. Her life consists of sitting in a chair or lying in bed. She cannot read, she cannot watch television. She just sits or sleeps. More to the point, she knows her condition. She wants to die and says so frequently. She also knows that she is a severe financial burden to her children, costing them about $8,000 per year. Upon every visit, after the usual niceties, she will say without bitterness or self-pity: I have had a good life, enjoyed it all, but now I am at the end, and it's time to go; I wish the Lord would take me tonight.

So there is the question: Why not? There are several ethical principles that argue against any mercy killing, and we have noted some of these before: "Thou shalt not kill"; "Only God has the right to take life"; "One should try to preserve life." There are also practical arguments such as the possible discovery of a new medicine that would relieve or partly solve the decay or disease; or that nature often comes up with recessive turns or sudden stops in deterioration; and that the abuses that would occur if mercy killing were legalized would be enormous. These arguments must be balanced with other ethical norms such as the desire of the patient, the suffering and deprivation of the children, the quality of life that is being "endured," and the general application of "the most loving thing to do." Attention must also be paid to the

practical problems of decision and control if euthanasia is to
be permitted.

Thus, a case for geriatric mercy killing can be made on
these secondary ethical principles: the suffering of the patient, the meaninglessness of her life now (or the quality of
it), her desire to die, the anguish and economic severity of
support. The primary principle involved is loving concern. A
conclusion can be reached that it would be a loving thing to
do to put her to sleep, to hasten the decaying process of death.
The practical problems of checking on the economics of the
family and its anguish, the medical diagnosis and administration of the medicine, the number and type of persons who
should be involved in the decision, could all be worked out
in a number of ways. For instance, agreement on the medical
facts by at least two or three doctors could be required; a
family lawyer (or two) should be present; three adult family
members, two neighbors, two or three other persons represent-
ing the state should be included in the decision. Or a review
board comprised of similar professional and family representatives could be defined and established. Protection for the
doctor who carried out the form of euthanasia would also be
required. Some consideration of the possible effect on relatives would be needed. All these are practical moral problems
which do involve risks and possible abuse. Yet one should not
fail to act because of possible misuse. Whatever the practical
difficulties might be, they must be measured against the weight
of the caring concern and ethical principles that aid the patient and her friends and relatives.

It might be helpful to note some common arguments used
against euthanasia, arguments that I believe are invalid, even
though some of them are couched in religious terms. One
sometimes hears the phrase, "It is the will of God," and the
implication is that one should not interfere with the final end
of a person's life. This phrase is a version of the phrase "Only
God has the right to take a life." It is implied, in the case of
an elderly person, that it is God's will that the person suffer

through a "vale of tears." Therefore, one should not interfere with the process of life and death.

Another argument is that such suffering is "the test of character." This view, which was old in Job's time, often asserts that God is helping the patient, or his relatives, by means of the ordeal to become more sensitive or religious or spiritual.

A third common argument is the ancient injunction, "Let nature take its course." Often there is a kind of quasi identification of God with natural process. This assumption is similar to the first argument, namely, that in euthanasia man is interfering against nature and therefore against God.

My response to these three common views is basically that they represent bad theology and poor ethics. It is bad theology to equate God with the process of nature. This kind of pantheism inevitably involves God with disease, disasters, and other monstrous evils of nature. To assert that God specifically and purposely causes awful suffering in order to make either the patient tougher morally or the observers of the agony more religious is to come up with a God who is a sadist, not a God of love. There is enough suffering and mystery and love and evil mixed up in life without creating a sadistic God in order to solve a problem.

To reject those three common views does not mean that there is no valid objection to euthanasia. We have already noted several valid ethical principles that can be used against mercy killing. And in any given specific example, I would recognize the possibility and the likelihood that equally loving and honest Christians might come to opposite conclusions. And this leads to the basic summaries of this section on problems of personal ethics.

Conclusions and Emphases

1. I believe it is a mistake to make into a dogmatic criterion any general ethical principle or natural law principle. To do so is often to pose false alternatives such as: Are you

for or against euthanasia, for or against the taking of human life? In absolutizing such principles one inevitably makes them into a rigid God, and the defender tends to sacrifice human concerns for the sake of "authority" or "tradition" or principle itself. Similarly, in attacking or denying the principles, one inevitably tends to make absolutes of antinomian motifs such as "conscience" or "the individual" or "freedom of self." And in the administration of either private action or a vague love-without-principles, the attacker also tends to sacrifice other persons and institutions to his "cause." In both cases, ethical principles are misused; in both instances idolatry is committed, i.e., a particular reality is regarded as the absolute reality. Idolatry is a strong and serious charge, yet it must be made and faced. Strong language is needed to combat the rigidities and self-righteousness that inevitably result from the practice of idolatry.

2. I believe we must affirm with equal strength again and again that there are general ethical and natural principles which all rational men can recognize and agree upon. But the proper place and use of these principles is *under* the one and only absolute—God and his love.

3. I believe it is thoughtfully obvious that many times several ethical principles may be in conflict with one another—e.g., mercy vs. justice, forgiveness vs. penance, sacrifice of life vs. saving life, dying for a cause vs. letting the cause die to save the people. When conflicting principles appear, the two decisive factors in selecting the "right" principle are: love and the "situation."

4. In the process of selection and application of principles it must be recognized that assessment of the "situation" will often vary and therefore, differences among Christians and others is to be expected. This should further underline the need for humility, and the necessity of spelling out how one is to make his moral decision.

5. The highly sensitive and debatable issues of sexuality, birth control, and euthanasia were especially chosen in order

to highlight these control problems. To illustrate once again in summary form: I believe it is erroneous and misleading to pose the question, Is suicide moral or immoral? (Substitute sexual intercourse, euthanasia, artificial contraception, killing deliberately.) Posing the question in that form assumes that suicide is a general problem with a general and abstract natural ethical answer. It further assumes that the answer pro or con can be arrived at abstractly. Once one introduces the qualifying phrase, "Well, it depends on the situation," then the problem is opened up for diverse applications, exceptions, other principles, and the standard used for their selection. This brings us back to the problems of authority, the Bible, infallibility, and the like—just where we belong. So what is our answer to the question of suicide? There will be several Christian answers: in most situations, one should not take his own life because to do so is a misuse of God's gift, because it involves an unlovely hatred-of-self motive and action, and because it is an expression of one's not loving friends or society, in that one fails to contribute or help. However, suicide could also be "the loving thing" for an elderly parent to do when faced with painful, slow mental and physical degeneration; when to continue living would be to burden his or her children with enormous costs, both economic and psychological; when it is no longer possible to contribute anything to anyone else or to society. All kinds of variations on both sides of the problem could be offered. The point is that *the* decisive factors are love and the situation, in addition to those principles which were deemed applicable and illuminative. In either case we have not solved the problem of authority. And this leads to our final emphasis and conclusion.

6. I believe there is no absolute ethical authority except God. Since by definition all else is less than God, no one and no institution can claim equality and exact identification with him. "There is only one God and there is *none* beside him." This means that in ethical decisions and moral actions one can never be sure that his action is 100 percent right, and one

ought to be aware that he, as a person, is not 100 percent righteous. From this it follows that the real purpose of Christian ethics and natural law principles should be to define as clearly as possible the nature of our ethical problems and moral choices. The purpose should be to define the mixtures of good and evil, right and wrong. The purpose of ethics and morals is *not* to guide us to righteousness or to assure us that we have done the right thing. The function of ethics is definition and analysis, identifying relevant principles, clarifying problems, and describing situations. By contrast, it is one of the functions of theology, prayer, and worship to forgive and renew us, and if there is any righteousness in us, that certainly comes from the Almighty and not from us.

Social Ethics

It is now my task to analyze some sample problems in the area of social ethics. It is hoped that such an analysis will further clarify the relationship between absolute love and general and natural law ethical principles, as well as their application to concrete moral situations.

But first I must establish the validity of this enterprise. To many schools of thought, such an endeavor might seem unnecessary. One such group might be the pietists. Pietism has had a long history, especially within Protestantism. It is the belief that religion should be concerned only with the individual and personal relationship between man and God. The chief function of religion is the cultivation of one's spiritual life. This means that one should *not* "mix politics and religion." It is part of the pietist's faith that his spiritual life should be kept apart from his business, political, or economic life. Similarly, the business of the church is worship and cultivation of the spiritual life; the job of the politician or entrepreneur is to run the state and the economy, and neither should interfere with the other. A recent letter to *The Washington Post* from a Maryland minister expressed this view neatly. "Let us

pray that the Lord will raise up more spiritual ministers and
better qualified statesmen, and like East and West, let the
twain never meet." [16]

My response to this pietistic view is first of all to observe
that it represents a protest against the abuses of religious
"interference" in politics and of the church "messing around"
in something it doesn't know anything about. I would agree
on the need for criticism. However, to bring about separation
and silence does not seem to be an adequate answer to the
misuse of roles. If the statesman and minister never meet, the
politician thereby will escape informed ethical criticism and
the clergyman will remain in his political ignorance. It is
also a bit ironic that many religious folk who complain the
loudest about the immorality of politics are exactly the same
ones who insist that the church keep silent about political
issues, saying: "Give us something spiritual, Reverend!" The
net ethical effect of that advice should be translated: "Give us
something comfortably irrelevant, Reverend."   *167819*

Another view that sees no significant relationship between
religious ethics and nuclear policy is the secular game theory.
This approach is essentially an attempt to produce a scientific
system for analyzing the many variables of possible strategies.
Thus, various "scenarios" and "games" are set up and programmed into computers, and results are thereby determined.
For example, a strategist might want to know what would be
the tactical cost if the enemy "took out" Chicago, Boston, and
Dallas. Could we survive economically and militarily? Should
we respond to the blackmail threat by "taking out" Leningrad,
Minsk, and two silos?

It is easy to imagine how "interesting" and technical such
"scenarios" can become. It is also easy to see how such a
system can overlook human and moral dimensions. Indeed,
when one reads such analyses, one often finds statements to
the effect that "only fifteen million people" would be killed
by Plan 4, or that we could survive an attack which cost
twenty million lives, "but probably not much more than that."

Yet no one seems to raise the fundamental ethical questions: Who decides that twenty million is the cut-off figure for tolerance? and by what criteria will such decisions be made? Who says Plan 4 is workable because it would sacrifice *only* fifteen million people?

A more profound and relevant reply to both the systems analyst and the pietist involves spelling out the fuller implications of gospel love. This means, among other things, that we are to obey the command "Feed my sheep," to deal with the whole man, to refuse to chop up life into isolated parts —economic and military, spiritual and material. The wider applications of Christian love have been well covered by many theologians, Catholic and Protestant alike.[17] For our purposes let us simply highlight and recall the relevant points: Love means caring about what happens to people. If they are in hunger, enslaved, exploited, sick and in prison, love means that we ought to help them. *How* help is most efficiently provided is the area of legitimate and necessary debate. But it is irresponsible simply to say: "The *how* is solely the job of the state," or "I will pray for the poor but I won't interfere." Everyone is aware of the past evils of the church when it identified the Kingdom of God with a particular king or cause or crusade. But again, the answer to those evils is not found in the opposite sins of inaction and irresponsibility. The problem is *how* to apply Christian love to specific social ethical situations, and that should now bring us back to the chief theme of this section: the relationships of love and principles and situations and people.

War

All informed Christians know that there are at least two legitimate ethical positions on war: the pacifist and the nonpacifist. It is not necessary to describe them here, nor is anything proved by arguing as to which came first in Christian history. Suffice it to say that the pacifist, nonviolent witness against all war is an authentic and needed Christian stance. Similarly, the discernment and participation in relatively just wars against brutal tyrants is also a valid Christian response. But now, with the advent of atomic and hydrogen bombs and other "doomsday devices," we must examine anew both classical Christian positions. While the historical views may still have relevance in contemporary nonatomic wars, the context is different. I must therefore analyze the "new situations" but not try to cover the whole range of problems involved. In my judgment the best book on these issues, whether one agrees with the author or not, is Paul Ramsey's *War and the Christian Conscience*.[18] I shall only highlight a few examples to test and illustrate my theses.

Atomic War. At first glance, it would seem obvious that all Christians would automatically be against atomic warfare. If by the word "atomic" one means full-scale hydrogen obliteration of a whole nation and the inevitable poisoning of its closest neighbors, then all Christians ought to be against such a war. By no situationalist application of love could one assert that "the loving thing to do" is to annihilate, for example, 250 million people (the population of Russia) in order to save some from Communism or tyranny. Whatever the issues may be, it is difficult to see how 250 million intentional deaths can outbalance even such causes as the preservation of democracy, our country, or our freedom. There are neither natural law principles nor ethical ideals which justify the slaughter of so great a number of innocent people. No matter how vicious a tyrant or political party in any country may be, the other people who live under such a jurisdiction cannot all be guilty enough to deserve being annihilated by atomic bombs, nor can we ever be righteous enough to decide that they do deserve it. Furthermore, as Ramsey points out, there is nothing in Christian ethics that justifies killing the "bad man's children" in order to restrain or punish him.[19] Even more serious, however, is the assumption behind this example. If we are talking about our killing 250 million people ("the enemy"), we are so far only talking about a preventive war and a first-strike attack. Clearly there are no ethical principles within Christianity that would justify such a move. A preemptive total strike assumes that one knows for sure that the enemy is about to launch a total-annihilation attack on us; therefore, we exclude the possibility of that attack by striking first. The truth is that we do not and could not know of such an attack in advance. To be sure, the superpowers have such doomsday plans, and weapons and systems to launch them. But prior to any such launch, there is no way anyone can know for a fact that such an attack will occur. And even if many "blips" were to appear on our radar screens, no one could know whether they indicated a selective first strike or a total-annihilation attack. In either case, there is no possible application of love or justice or natural law principles which could conclude that it is morally right (or even the lesser of two evils) to take the initiative and engage in a wholesale obliteration of a population called "the enemy." By contrast, *all* the Christian and human principles of love, justice, moral discernment, and the like would be against any such decision. Does anyone believe that a person in his right mind could justify intentional killing of 250 million people on the supposition that their armed forces *might* bomb us *someday?* Here, for once, is the opportunity for a straightforward and unequivocal answer: a huge and decisive NO!

But now let us complicate the simplicity of a NO to atomic annihilation by raising the problem of nuclear deterrence as a possible valid policy toward preserving a tenuous peace. We are now talking about the present situation. Our situation is that the superpowers all have atomic weapons. Each has the capacity to annihilate the others, and the whole world, if madness took over. This mutual death threat acts as a mutual restraining power. The basic problem for any responsible policymaker is how to preserve the balance of deterrent forces in order to preserve a minimal balance of "peace" and order, or (to put it another way) how to avoid a devastating invasion or war. One of the key items in this awesome juggling of counterforces is the possibility of selective strike power plus the threat of total annihilation. Specifically this means that a nation must maintain a reasonable balance of power with its potential enemies. At the same time, it must have "contingency plans" that would enable it to have both selective and second-strike capacity. There is a little black case (or "football" as it is called) carried by an unostentatious man who follows the President wherever he goes. Inside the "football" are electronic keys specifically designed to give launch signals to atomic missiles for *predesignated selective targets*. It is significant that the case does not have just two buttons: one for no, and one for yes, meaning all-out destruction. Most of it is constructed for selective and restrained targets. This assumes that an enemy might try to blackmail or threaten us into some agreement by selectively striking one or two cities or silos. If such a disaster occurred, our choice would be to surrender to the enemy's demands or to threaten to or actually strike back and wipe out two of their comparable cities or sites. Such a posture might induce more peaceful negotiations. It might also escalate to the ultimate risk of total annihilation. Consider the dilemma of a President or high policymaker in the hypothetical case that our nation is threatened with complete extinction. Negotiations, other means, and even a few selective strikes are tried, and all fail. The enemy threat is clear and absolute: give in, or die. Obviously, it is a defensible position to agree to surrender. This would be the standard pacifist position. It would also be realistic, pragmatic action such as many small European nations have taken over the past fifty years. There may be a few patriots who would shout, "Give me liberty or give me death." But when faced with overwhelming power, most people will reluctantly and sadly go the way of Czechoslovakia, Hungary, and Bulgaria, or of Latvia, Estonia, and Lithuania.

There is, however, one other moral choice possible, and that is to counter the extinction threat with its identical counter annihilation power. This sort of ultimate threat and identical counter power now already exist. Russia and the United States know that each country could destroy the other. Thus, if a situation is reached where one nation could destroy or enslave the other without fear of retaliation, that nation might just do one of these things. It is assumed, therefore, that when another nation maintains nearly equal power it thereby reduces that temptation. But the critical problem still must be faced: Suppose the total threat is made. What shall be our response? The answer of the realist is: We must threaten, nay, guarantee that if we are destroyed, they will be destroyed.

That is a realistic answer. Can a Christian adopt such a position, and if so, how? Beginning at the end rather than with the prior principles, let me state what I believe is *a* valid Christian response to this awful choice. If faced with a real blackmail threat of surrender or total annihilation, I believe the Christian may also threaten the blackmailer with return extinction: if you annihilate us, we'll annihilate you. As noted above, it is this kind of mutual terror which may prevent (and has in part so far prevented) atomic warfare. In political terms, the possession of power and the threat of its use can, in fact, prevent war. The means do not hurt anybody; the end or goal is "nonwar" (i.e., an uneasy, tenuous peace). The risks are enormous, for there is no guarantee that this power balance and mutual threat will not escalate, or that one side will not miscalculate the seriousness of the other. And there is always the possibility of an unintentional electronic mistake. This latter point, however, is a given risk and is ever present in an atomic age regardless of any specific threat, enemy, or policy. In this regard it is significant to note that in twenty-five years the automobile has killed over two million people and injured ten million. A small nuclear attack would produce about the same casualties. We seem to be willing to live with the actual deaths rather than abolish the automobile. Similarly, we can run the *risk* of atomic death in order to defend certain values and seek more creative uses of atomic energy.

But back to our basic problem: we are asserting Christian agreement with the "realist" position of maintaining a relatively equal balance of power and of countering a blackmail threat of total annihilation with an equal threat of extinction. Yet there is one nearly absolute difference that must be faced. It is this: if the mutual threats did not preserve the tenuous "peace," and if an enemy did let go and virtually annihilate us, would we "press the buttons" and "let them have it in return"? The Christian answer to this situation must be: *"No— but never tell the enemy that you won't!"*

What is the basis for the NO? One reason would be that one does not kill the entire population of a nation just because their tyrannical government is evil. Secondly, even if that evil government killed all of our 210 million people, what would be the point in atomizing all of its 250 million people? If we have been extinguished, our nation is gone, we are dead, there is nothing left. Assuming that there is somebody left down in the "situation room" at the White House or the President and his "football" are in the air over Alaska and therefore the all-out button can be pushed, what would be the point of wiping out another entire nation of 250 million people? If one could selectively kill only the enemy tyrant and his cohorts, that might be permissible. But that is not the choice. So we must stay with the hard terms of our example. And so I would reaffirm the NO. To kill all of them because all of us have beeen killed is vengeance. To this, the Christian must say NO.

Now what about the "but"? What about the condition: *"but don't tell the enemy you won't be vengeful."* The point of the "but" is obvious. If one publicly announces that we have the means and the power for total destruction, but that we will never use it, even if we are eliminated, is to divest oneself of the very power one has. There would be no point in even building such power at all; there would be no balance, no protection. In this case if one were openly honest about the intended use of power, one would lose that power. Instead, the Christian is put into the fantastically ambiguous situation of maintaining the ultimate power of destruction, knowing that he would never use it for total extinction, but publicly denying such limits. The tiniest comfort he might receive is the probability that no one would believe him. It is this kind of mix of awesome power, the possibility of appalling killing, the ethical complexity and the theoretical absurdity of it all, that is enough to make one flee into the simplicities of pacifism or seek out a cave or a pond where one can find a "back to nature" escape.

This is precisely why we have chosen this kind of problem. Again, let it be emphasized that the Christian pacifist non-violent position is still a valid one. There are three things to remember about it: (1) It is unlikely that any present nation will voluntarily adopt it. (2) It is impossible to run any state on pacifist principles, internally or externally. (3) The chief weakness of this view is that it often does little to restrain tyranny (internal or external) or to rescue its victims, so this is not a "pure position." Humility becomes the pacifist as it becomes all of us.

At this point another emphasis should be made. In the chapter dealing with theology I argued that all of us need a renewed sense of God as the Lord and the judge of history, that there is a moral order to the major events in history and that nations and peoples must pay attention to such realities or suffer lawful reactions. One of the ways of applying such apparently vague theological statements is to see that such a horrendous situation exists because of our respective moral failures to find more just and peaceable solutions. Our internal evils of corruption, exploitation, and racism have brought on domestic malaise, insecurity, and apathy. Similarly, our international policies of mutual arrogance, violence, and ruthless insults to the Third World peoples have led the superpowers to this abyss of mutual nuclear fear. The abuse of our power has made us victims of its terror. Life is not meant to be lived this way. This is not God's will or love for mankind, that men should threaten each other with such death. But since we seem to have violated the structures of history and the more just ways, we have brought this situation upon ourselves.

It is in this context, I believe, that such an awesome nuclear threat must be viewed. In a very real sense this is a terrible example to pose. But two more points need to be made about this truly "hellish" situation. First, it is a *real* situation, not a frivolous scenario. Consider, for example, the Mideast crisis of October 25, 1973. Our National Security Council unanimously believed that the Russians were about to or might send some troops into Egypt. President Nixon ordered a nuclear alert of the Strategic Air Command in addition to various troop alerts. Here was an actual nuclear threat in response to a possible land occupation of a very small part of Egypt. Suppose Russia had responded with a similar nuclear alert aimed at us? What would the President have done if he had thought Russia intended to land on our soil, not in faraway Egypt? Would he have called for an alert or an actual atomic bombing? Why didn't he use the "hot line" and call Moscow on that potentially fateful Thursday night? My point is that we are already in this awesome, "hellish" situation.

Secondly, in the face of such gruesome choices and possibilities one is tempted to say: "Well, a Christian shouldn't get himself into such situations. Maybe it is not possible to be a President or a politician or a businessman and be a Christian at the same time." In response to such an understandable reaction I would point out that if Christian ethics are only applicable to the "good" situations in life, then they are but frail reeds. To those who ask whether one could imagine Christ being a bombardier, or a president of Boeing, or of the United States, I would answer that such a question is beside the point. It is not our purpose to imitate the vocation of

Jesus; otherwise we should all have to be "sometime car-
penters." The real vocation of Jesus Christ was to reveal the
nature of God, which he did by his words, deeds, and life.
And because of that life, we know that the will of God for
us is to love and do justice wherever we are.

Similarly, it would have been tempting and much easier
for me to have chosen an easier social issue to test our model.
How relatively simple it would be to ask: Should we send
wheat to starving India, or medical and technological help to
the new nations in Africa? And if so, by what principles does
one decide what economic and psychological situations need
to be considered? Probably everyone would agree that we
should send help, though there might be some minor disagree-
ments as to the most efficient ways of doing so, considering
national sensitivities of freedom and pride. But it would be a
fairly easy ethical choice. If so, then the test of the model on
the relevance of Christian ethics to the harsh realities of
modern life would be suspect.

So let us stay with the most difficult example: Let us see if
Christian ethics can offer any help in the most ghastly of situations at the edge of the abyss. Let us return to the Christian
nonpacifist position and see whether or not we can now adequately explain how one gets "from here to there," from love
to the threat of atomic annihilation. Indeed that is where we
start, and love is to be our guiding principle and motivating
force. Under love comes the "orders of creation"—the natural
law requiring some form of social and political order. In order
to avoid chaos, hunger, and slavery, some minimal state is
necessary. If the state is threatened with extinction or slavery,
it must have some effective power to thwart attackers from
the outside and to preserve or achieve justice from within.
If the problem becomes one of conflict between two states—as
in our monstrous example—then we shall also have to draw
upon the ethical tradition of natural law.

It might be useful to list briefly the classical seven criteria
for a "just war," which are derived from Augustine (*City of*

God XIX) and Thomas Aquinas (*Summa Theologica* IIa IIae. 40).

1. The war must be declared by legitimate public authority in the country that goes to war.
2. The injury or injustice that the war is intended to prevent or rectify must be real and certain.
3. The seriousness of the injury must be proportional to the damages that the war will cause.
4. There must be reasonable hope of success in waging the war.
5. Hostilities may be initiated only as a last resort.
6. A war may be prosecuted legitimately only insofar as the responsible agents have a right intention.
7. The particular measures used in conducting the war must themselves be moral.

In the use of these seven criteria, as with all other guiding principles, it is the overall intent and "spirit" that can be helpful. A rigid, literalistic application would destroy the kind of ethic I am working to develop. For example, if criterion number 1 were applied to the Vietnam war in a legalistic way, we could say: The United States never made public declaration of war; therefore, our presence and our fighting in Vietnam was illegal and unjust. That probably is technically and literally true. However, if that were the *only* injustice we committed, and given the obvious injustices of the Viet Cong, that one criterion would not be sufficient to condemn the war as unjust.

By contrast, when one applies all seven criteria, it is a valid judgment that the Vietnam war has been an unjust war. The most serious violations we engaged in were criteria numbers 2, 3, 4, and 7. The extent and intent of the various policies and deeds can and should be debated, and there are many earlier "ifs" and "buts" that enter in. In any case, I believe the Vietnam war illustrates how the criteria for a just war can be importantly valid and necessary. I would even argue that had they been used earlier and more widely, they might have helped us to avoid many of the evils we unwittingly committed.

Similarly, I believe these seven criteria are still relevant to the problems of atomic war. I have already recommended Ramsey's book[20] for its typical examples. We are now suggesting that the criteria are even applicable to our "doomsday" example. For instance, the just war theory is clearly against total destruction. Criteria numbers 4 and 7 are particularly forceful. Number 4 states that there must be a reasonable hope of success in waging the war. The "success hoped for" would be the avoidance of both our own and the enemy's total extinction. If the enemy succeeds in destroying 210 million Americans (owing to our lack of power or the threat of it, or for some other reason), then there is no goal or ideal or point in killing 250 million Russians. Criterion number 7 calls for the use of moral measures in the conduct of the war. Surely no one could assert that vengeful "let's get 'em" extinction is moral. And what would be "the right intention" (number 6) of a total reprisal bombing? Thus, I believe the just war theory clearly asserts the NO to a complete first strike and a retaliation strike *in toto*.

Next, how does the theory support the pretense that we would engage in such a total reprisal? The criteria all support the use of power to maintain or achieve justice and social order. But now we find ourselves in a crucial "crunch." We are faced with atomic blackmail and the threat of our 210 million people being destroyed. What shall we do? I would argue that a conscious and deliberate lie, even such a lie publicly and internationally proclaimed, must be balanced against the saving of 210 million people. In such a balance, it seems to me that the people clearly come first. Love of the people vs. the principle of honesty and my integrity is one issue; but the second issue is that there are also the other principles of social justice, resistance to tyranny and blackmail that are in force here. One must note the conflict of several ethical principles: honesty vs. conscious deception, pretense vs. social justice. Yet one must then ask: if a country engages in deliberate deception at this highest level, what happens to its credibility and integrity at lower and less awesome levels? Will other nations ever trust us at all? But this argument can also be reversed and made to support the effectiveness of our original position. That is, if we are honest and credible on most of our secondary and important promises and commitments, and are "realistic" in our power balance actions, then our ultimate pretense becomes more effective and credible. The final moral irony is that the more credible our deception, the less likely it will ever have to be discovered. By contrast, if we were unrealistic in our use of power, gave in easily to lower-level types of threat and blackmail, were notoriously noble and "soft," then an enemy might very easily conclude that it could successfully enslave us precisely because we were so "good" and so moral that we would never even threaten him, let alone use atomic missiles. This is the partial validity of "the Munich syndrome": Hitler could successfully enslave Austria and Czechoslovakia because he knew the Allies were unable (realistically) to stop him and unwilling (morally) to do so.

We are now trying to conclude that it is a valid Christian moral position to agree with the "realist" in a tactic of penultimate atomic blackmail in which we say "no" to total reprisal—but don't tell anybody. Humanely speaking, the most important application of love is to ask: What course is necessary for saving most lives? Theoretically and ideally, the pacifist strategy is the best and the most obvious. But the ideal and theoretical option is not open to us. If a country is small and has little power, it must surrender and be enslaved if confronted by a powerful invader. Such surrender is usually effected not by voluntary Christian pacifist nonviolent idealism, but by inevitable and regretful realism. But if the situation is between two superpowers, as it is in our example of the

United States vs. Russia, then the choices are different. The pacifist strategy is the reminder of the weaknesses of our nonpacifist position. The only other choices are the tactical ones between the ruling realists, and any influence we Christian and other, similar "realists" may have upon the present policymakers and our culture. Given that "situation," our problem is to decide what is the most loving (and therefore human) thing to do. Thus I want to stress two major points in the conclusion of this ethical section on the problem of war.

First, I have deliberately chosen a most difficult, complex, and awesome moral dilemma to illustrate that a combination of the two Christian ethical traditions of love and natural law can be helpful and applicable. I have tried to outline how one can get "from here to there," how one's motive and ambience is love guided by many ethical principles. Obviously, I have not resolved every operative rule or possible alternative, but have only tried to develop some sample problems. It should be equally obvious that the conclusion reached is not the only Christian possibility. Our only contention is that it is a valid Christian decision. Other Christian "realists" might assess the variables differently and come to another decision. For instance, a President must maintain a balance of power but draw the line on atomic bombing by allowing its use for the bombing of missile sites only, never for the bombing of cities, no matter what the threat—even the loss of some of our cities. But again, our emphasis is to point out how the decisions can be made by the use of many principles, selected by love and reason, and related to even the most horrendously complicated power situations. To announce that there is a valid Christian way of making such awesome decisions is not new. If we stopped here, we would end up with the usual justification for a moral action. The decision maker might be grateful to us. Whoever made the policy could feel righteous, and we would be right back where we started, i.e., at providing an ethical system that is both relevant and righteous, and which offers us an easy conscience. So we cannot stop here.

Yet I want to insist on the value of dealing with the *how*. Its value is that Christian ethics can be made relevant and realistic to the most complex of moral problems.

Now I must confess the limits and weaknesses of the *how*, and why an uneasy conscience is the only proper stance at the end of the decision. Granted the relevance and the rightness of the fateful decisions, what are the issues involved which are also relevant but wrong? What immoral or unethical principles are we committing? If we start with our love absolute, we know that our national policies may not work, and if they do not, millions of people will be killed. While the policy may work and thereby no one is destroyed, there is no guarantee of "success," and we cannot, therefore, simply offer to "personally apologize" if millions of people are destroyed. While one cannot refrain from acting because of possible dangers, the vast number of casualties, if failure occurs, is almost overwhelming. This has to be balanced, however, by the human lives that are affected if one "gives in" or consents to an unrestricted weapons race. One can avoid the decisions by resigning or assigning them to someone else. But in our example, we are assuming that the policymaker will stay in office and shoulder his responsibilities. So one relevant help is criterion number 4, that of "a reasonable hope of success." Since mutual atomic deterrence has worked, however precariously, so far there are considerable "reasonable" grounds for continuing this policy. Nevertheless the risk factor and the horrendous price of failure must be ever present in the conscience of the decision maker.

Additional weaknesses and immoralities in our example should be stressed. We engaged in deliberate pretense. We will lie if necessary. If we are asked whether we will retaliate in kind in the event of a full-scale attack, we will reply in the affirmative. And if we privately believe we will not "push the button," we shall have to make great efforts to deny this, to establish the credibility of our claim that we are not lying. This will lead to other problems regarding the government's credibility. In addition, if we continue to adopt the balance-of-power strategy, we may get caught in an arms escalation which we neither want nor believe in. If Russia or China (or both) develop new defenses against our present delivery system, presumably we would have to spend billions to invent new missiles. And of course, the other superpowers will feel the same way. President Nixon used to emphasize that the United States must be number one. This is to discard balance in favor of superiority. It will work if nobody else wants to or is able to challenge us. Since the other superpowers are able to be number one if they want to, escalation is inevitable. But even if an equal balance is sought, escalation is also inevitable unless the superpowers agree to that equal balance. Since this would be difficult to achieve, another alternative might be uni-laterally to stop escalating. Since we have enough to kill every-body now, why increase the overkill? The chief difficulty with this proposal would be getting our own country to agree to it —a dubious possibility—and then trying to get Russia to be-lieve we meant it. In any case, one can see how feeble are the alternatives to an escalated balance-of-power strategy.

Therefore we must ask, what is the danger of continuing the balance-of-power policies? The dangers lie in the awesome escalation with all its frightful perils, economic costs, and waste. It also means a further intensification of the whole "military-industrial complex" and its weaknesses. This is not to say that such a complex is all evil or that bigness is bad *per se*. But there is no doubt, as President Eisenhower recog-nized, that there are inherent evils which have their own momentum and structure that make it almost impossible to control or reform. The present spasmodic on-again, off-again appropriations and cutbacks in space, military, and medical research are an inefficient and even, at times, disastrous way to try to meet these problems. Analogically speaking, a scien-tist cannot do effective research on alternate weeks, or every other month, or only during odd years.

What I am trying to summarize is that in point one, we

have offered the best, or one of the best Christian-realistic decisions that can be made within the present system. Now, here in point two, we are noting the weaknesses, and one of the biggest dangers is that we are doing almost nothing to change the "system." In fact, our decision tends to maintain the system. Clearly the system is not all bad. Nevertheless, we are doing little to reform its immoralities; we are, in some ways, strengthening or continuing them. In Chapter VII we shall discuss this type of problem more in detail. Suffice it to say here that I am noting this issue as a major weakness in the "realist" approach.

Finally, I must acknowledge that, unless our hypothetical policymaker was providing leadership to reduce international tensions and internal conflicts, his penultimate decision by itself would be hard to defend. If our President at the time was increasing our foreign problems by involvement in new Vietnams, or in "bomb-rattling diplomacy," asking for wild weaponry appropriations to the neglect of social problems such as the ghetto, then in this kind of atmosphere his decision would surely be credible, but whether it would be moral would be quite debatable.[21] But even if there were a better moral atmosphere, this sample atomic decision still has much evil and precarious risk in it.

If we add these two conclusions together, we have a picture of a man faced with a fantastically complex and awesome problem, but a man who has used the best resources of the Christian ethical tradition. He therefore has "done the best he can," chosen "the lesser of two evils," made a valid "Christian-realistic choice," and achieved "the loving thing to do in the situation." Yet he is also a man who, because he has such enormous power and therefore enormous responsibility, should be extremely humble and uneasy. He should be humble in the sense that he is aware that he is not always right. It is essential for him to look inward for weaknesses and evils that might be corrected or changed. He is uneasy because he has to steer clear of self-righteousness without overlooking the immoralities he has both committed and been forced to continue. If one is aware of only his goodness, he will be insufferable and undo us all; if one is aware of only his evils, he will be helpless and aid us not at all.

Violence

There is little doubt that all kinds of violence have increased in America over the last ten years. And with this phenomenon has appeared a lot of violent rhetoric and contradictory responses. Some representatives of the radical left have railed against our violence in Vietnam but called for bombing and violence at home. Some of the radical right have cried out against the violence of the leftists, but themselves have wanted to "get those niggers" and believe they "should have shot more of those kids" (the latter a quote from the famous Kent State University case). Others, in the middle of the political spectrum, seem to feel that if someone has been the victim of violence, he is entitled to retaliate with violence. Most of us are familiar with other illustrations of loose rhetoric and wild examples of violence.

It would seem appropriate in the face of this rising problem to have a brief look at how Christian ethics might make a contribution toward understanding and controlling violence in our times. Obviously in this small book I cannot cover all aspects nor do full justice to the issues. Hence, I have a few examples as illustrations.

If we begin with our Christian absolute of love, then our primary concern is for the victims of violence. As Christians, we are supposed to care about what happens to people. Therefore, our first response should be toward those who are the sufferers of violence. From this it follows that the next step is how to help the victims and protect them from further harm. When we introduce the *how* of helping we are also introducing "the situation" and what effective guiding principles are at hand. Our natural law resources tell us that the primary moral validity of force, violent or nonviolent, is its use to restrain an unjust force.[22] The moral determination of what kind of force and how much force to use is determined in large part by the nature and use of the opposing force. Here again the criteria for a just war can be most helpful. The chief aim is the saving and protecting of life. By definition, therefore, one uses only enough force to do the job. One does not restrain an unarmed robber by killing him with a machine gun or cannon. That is too much force, and because it kills, it is immoral. On the other hand, one does not reason with, and quote Jesus and Gandhi to, a murderous psychopath. The failure to use restraining force on such a person would be immoral, for one would fail to protect his victims.

These kinds of distinctions can be made under the guidance of natural law principles informed by love. Further distinctions also need to be made in our culture. Categories such as nonviolent vs. violent force are not enough. As we all know, there are many examples in which both types of force overlap. The assumption that nonviolent force is always better than violent force is not always correct. For example, a small amount of police strength at the right place and the right time may prevent a huge bloody riot; the same force at the wrong place and the wrong time may cause a riot. Similarly, insidious nonviolent propaganda may successfully destroy a man's character and career almost as effectively as if one shot him. Because the propaganda was nonviolent does not make it good.

So we need to draw upon man's reason and the natural law tradition to try to sort out as carefully as possible important and qualifying distinctions. We need to make clear that violence which kills is worse than violence which destroys property. People come before things. On the other hand, continuous economic exploitation of the ghetto poor *is* a special kind of violence which needs more moral attention as such. Precisely because such exploitation is so diffuse and subtle, it is hard to pinpoint. Yet it is so pervasive and gradually destructive that it needs more severe condemnation and action. If we more fully understood this phenomenon, we should not be so surprised that this kind of economic and psychological violence tends to breed physical violence.

Hubert Humphrey was especially sensitive and honest when, in his 1968 campaign, he admitted that if he had been brought up in some of the ghettos he had seen, he might have done some violent protesting himself. From our viewpoint, this does not make such violence good, but it should make us understand some of the "why" of its appearance. Another lesson that ghetto violence offers us is to point up the hypocrisy of many who are frightened at such physical violence and who then call for more "law and order." Yet some of these are the same persons who own the exploiting companies and shops in the ghetto, or who are the city planners who push for the superhighway or the new luxury high rise in the ghetto area. This results in "Negro removal," not "urban renewal," and only intensifies the lot of the poor—black and white.

The rising street violence in our cities also illustrates our failure to understand and deal with violence. Conservatives and middle-of-the-roaders tend to call for more "law and order" against the perpetrators of violent acts. "Shoot 'em first" is an increasingly common cry. Liberals and leftists, on the other side, tend to call for less force and more long-range sociological reform. The charge that liberals are often more concerned with reform of the criminals and prisons than they are with the victims is mostly true. There are many "liberal committees" for penal reform, for better justice for the criminals, or for "freeing political prisoners," yet there are few committees to aid the victims, most of whom are blacks, women, and elderly people. A more profound view of the nature of man, as well as prudent moral distinctions, should help us to see that all the problems are intertwined. One cannot solve violence in the streets simply by employing a larger police force or by spending more money in the ghetto areas. In our more rational moments we should know that the courts need reform as well as the police and the legislatures. Therefore, we have to work on all of the problems simultaneously. Meanwhile, I am suggesting that it will be helpful if we use the resources of our tradition to define and describe different types of force and violence, situations where they may be justly or unjustly used, the balancing of psychological violence vs. physical force, economic violence vs. propaganda violence, and so on.

While the Christian ideal is reform by love and persuasion, our doctrine of human sin informs us that force of all kinds is necessary to prevent evil and injustice. This is the ancient Augustinian insight. We need to be reminded that force can sometimes be used to achieve justice. As we all know, many people and institutions will not change voluntarily but only under the threat of or the use of the needed force. Force need not be violent. Court action, boycott, the power of tax, often will bring about reforms. Force, then, is necessary to prevent evil *and* to achieve justice.

Violence needs to be more clearly defined and limited to the area of destruction. If one destroys a life, there is no chance for reform or to correct the error of the action. Similarly, destruction of property is less evil than the killing of people. On the other hand, it is a serious evil because the reasons for such violence are seldom the property itself. It is usually an indirect action, i.e., it is a dramatic way of calling attention to one's purpose—whatever it may be. The act is therefore usually committed only after one's protest has been ignored. It may have other symbolic and hoped-for practical effects, but the moral seriousness of the act is twofold. First, some property has great social value, such as factories and transport and communications facilities. To destroy such buildings may seriously affect thousands of innocent people. Secondly, personal and private property, for example, like one's home, still seems to be a natural part of one's "right of livelihood." To destroy that is to attack one's place of living. On the other hand, it is difficult to give a high moral rating to the preservation of a mile of private beach while the public is jammed into a town beach of one hundred yards. An attack on, or destruction of, "minor property" has small value in itself. But what makes such violence have high moral seriousness is precisely not the property itself, but the purpose of the action *and* the fact that violence was used. We need to ask whether the amount and type of force used is justified by the amount of unjust force that one is opposing. Such a question leads into other distinctions such as economic and psychological force. Naturally, honest differences of assessment and balancing of relative values will occur. There will be no simple answer of yea or nay. Yet the effect of the process—regardless of the final moral decision—will, in itself, have a restraining effect on the use of force, particularly destructive violence.

The recent history of modern industrial labor strikes will illustrate our point. Previously, labor strikes were violent in that actual destruction of property was often involved. Labor would sometimes break machinery, or temporarily "fix" a machine so that it would not work. The company, in response, would sometimes try to break the strike, literally and physically, by sending in armed "goons" or police. Most of the damage was done therefore to company property and to the strikers. Nowadays, violence to strikers or destruction of company property is less frequent. But the damage done to the public is, in many cases, enormous. Because of our increasing economic interdependence, a small "wildcat strike" can seriously affect millions of people: thousands are laid off in jobs dependent upon, say, transportation of goods; hospitals cannot operate a special machine; food will be spoiled if not moved quickly. The proportion of violence to millions compared to the economic injustice to the strikers is often far out of balance. It is clear that we need a new set of definitions and analyses and the balancing of forces at work in our economic and political life. And it will not do just to lump all issues under violence and then deplore it all. In a later section I will deal with the difficult and basic problem of "reform within the system" vs. "change of the whole system." But, for the present, I only wish to emphasize my belief that a situational ethic based upon love-informed natural law can do a great deal to help our future handling of violence. Rome and Geneva's ethical alliance has much to contribute!

Racism

Racial problems in the United States of America in the late 1960's raised acutely the ancient ethical issue of ends and means. For one of the central slogans of the black militants was the declaration: "We shall achieve justice by *any* means necessary." This was a conscious and deliberate announcement that "whitey" could no longer count on the gentle restraint of Martin Luther King's nonviolent methods. This emphasis was accompanied by open and acknowledged purchase of weapons, and even a "rhetoric of the gun" was developed.[23] The blacks claim that their stockpiling of guns for defensive purposes only was not believed by the white communities.

Naturally, most white people recoiled in horror at this violent development. Racist fears were increased, and preparations for counterviolence were much more widespread than was publicized. But regardless of the reactions and the more intense polarization, the black militant emphasis on "by any and all means necessary" still raises an essential ethical dilemma. So our problem is: How shall we respond to this declaration? I believe we have to meet the issue on two levels. First, we must understand the problem on the "situational" level. Secondly, we can then deal with the matters more adequately on the theoretical level.

So let us begin on the situational level. As I have already noted, one reason for the "any means" declaration was to announce a new militancy and an impatience with nonviolent gradualism. This was part of the larger cultural problem of slow progress in racial justice and the appearance of more virulent racism in the North. As the blacks knew all along, racism was not just a southern problem. Faced with nationwide injustice, the blacks knew that new methods and tactics would have to be used if any progress was to be achieved. Further, the now familiar phrases "Black Power" and "Power to the People" were also used to emphasize the need for all kinds of power. It was, in part, a deliberate slogan to counter the earlier sweet, persuasive, rational approach. Black people knew that they could not overcome racial prejudice and injustice by reasonableness and "friendly persuasion."

Third, another reason for the "any means" strategy was both to scare and to warn whitey that anything goes in the struggle for liberation. This meant that whites and the Establishment could not count on any set strategy or behavior. "House niggers" and "oreos" (blacks who think as whites) were no longer the spokesmen and leaders for the black communities. White power would be met by black power; if there was white violence, there would be black violence in return, or maybe some other tactic of a different kind—a surprise: the threat of "Burn, baby, burn." At one moment there was a cool, incisive use of political or economic power; at another moment, any method that was appropriate to the situation would be used—and with complete justification. Such were the essential reasons behind this black announcement of "any means." Such was the cultural situation, in part.

The other part of the cultural situation will lead us to the theoretical level. This is the realistic problem of effectiveness. As we all know, the blacks announced that they were weary of three hundred years of slavery in America, tired of the slow progress in their behalf since the Civil War, and even worried about the regress in some parts of the North and Midwest. The tokenism of the 1940's and the integration of the 1950's seemed more like absorption into white, middle-class culture than equal justice and black freedom. The snail's pace of working within the system came to be endless and inefficient. And so many blacks came to the critical point of deciding that the system itself is repressive, reform from within is impossible, and therefore the whole system must be changed "by any and all means." Since there is abundant evidence that the system has used and will continue to use "any means" to keep itself intact, it is equally obvious that the blacks, or any people who want significant change, will *have* to counter with "any and all means." Something akin to this is the thinking and feeling of many black, as well as white, militants.

This, then, brings us to the ethical and theoretical response to the above situation. In general, we probably would have begun by quickly denying that a Christian could give a *carte blanche* to "any means." The Christian tradition (among others) has always insisted on relating ends and means, goals and methods, and affirming that a noble purpose does *not* justify all possible methods. That is to say, there are limits, or should be. What then shall we say to the militants? Mindful of our "one and only absolute" we cannot agree to an unrestrained, unlimited means. On the other hand, given "the situation," given the vast and vicious means by which blacks have been victimized, and given the desperate need for effective progress and relief from the urban ghettos, is it not at least a legitimate mix of good and evil to threaten "any means" against a superpowerful majority who already have used all devious and suppressive methods? I believe the threat as well as *some* unspecified differing means can be morally defended. There are, however, two limitations. One would be existentially tactical: What is most practical? What will work? If a tactic is counterproductive, abandon it. Secondly, I could not justify the torture of children, the poisoning of reservoirs, the bombing of subways or hospitals. On the other hand, if I am enslaved, I am not going to announce to my captors what methods I will *not* use. And if I am a leader with some charisma, I will not try to encourage and cheer on my brothers with a thousand qualifications. Inwardly, I would know and must know what I would *not* do.

The reader will note the similarity of this moral decision with that of the penultimate atomic war blackmail problem. There is public deceit here combined with personal integrity, and limits to both. There are even public social limits, for example, we would *not* destroy everything; but one does not publish that. There is also the credibility issue, and of course the blacks know in advance that their credibility is greatly enhanced by the racist. For it is the white racist who is sure that the black militant *will* destroy everything, torture children, "kill whitey," or rape his women. Thus, the white man's racist fears increase the effective credibility and power of the black, which is what is sought for in the first place. Of course, if the white man's fears lead him to counterattack with more repression, then the black will have to devise some other tactic.

Regardless of what tactic, threat, or action is decided upon, our primary emphasis must be on how such a decision was reached.

Two differing black Christian descriptions of how one moves from here to there, from the gospel to "any means" to freedom and justice, can be found in the works of J. Deotis Roberts and James H. Cone.[24] Both envision the gospel as proclaiming liberation: Roberts sees the need for limited means and ultimate reconciliation. Cone calls for "any means" and stops at liberation in his book. In conversation, however, Cone makes it very clear that his emphasis is tactical and situational. He, too, is for eventual reconciliation, but he believes (or believed in 1969, when he wrote his book) that the time is not ripe for such talk. "How can we be reconciled if we are not yet free?" In my judgment, both books are powerful, but both need more clarification as to how each author derives his position.

It is now my responsibility to suggest how one white Christian can proceed from the gospel to an "almost any means" decision. Love tells one that it is an obvious duty to care for all victims of injustice and exploitation. It is equally obvious that blacks have been and still are enslaved in many ways— socially and economically. Therefore love demands that we help. But how? This question leads one to check out various ethical and natural law principles: justice, equality, freedom, the rights of man. Thus, one would support all specific policies, bills, and programs that enhance these principles, however imperfect specific actions may be. Something is better than nothing. The "how" also leads one to inquire about the nature of the "situation." We have highlighted some of the cultural problems above. But other difficulties will surface, and one also needs to press on to the facts, the secular knowledge of the difficulties. Here we will learn, among other things, that just pouring money into renewal is not enough, that white bureaucratic planning is not good enough, that local black planning is not adequate, and so on. Eventually we will come to a crisis dilemma, which I will now describe.

If one believes that sufficient reform can be effected within the present system, he is faced with these vague but pervasive problems: the attitudes of racism are still deep in the majority of people all over the nation. Local governments are not likely to change very fast or very basically, particularly in the economic aspects of housing and equality of schooling; nobody really knows how to solve the ghetto problem. Therefore, any effective solution to all of these problems will require an enormous amount of pressure, billions of dollars, and a lot of mutual experimental programs that will guarantee nothing. To expect a widespread and huge effort for so tenuous a result strains credulity and one's belief in man's goodness. Our American pragmatism and our desire-for-success mentality usually demand visible results, a clear answer, and minimum cost. And our racism often aggravates this problem when, for example, we ourselves are quite willing to gamble on a business venture or on the horses or on conquering space; but just let a couple of welfare cheaters get caught and publicized, and we're ready to cut out the whole welfare appropriation. So, for those of us who believe in reform within the system, our gospel motive of love and the guidance of our several principles are severely limited by the present situation. The evidence for our realism and effectiveness is not very persuasive.

If one believes the present system is incapable of sufficient and basic liberation, then he must favor abolishing the system and replacing it with a better one. This, too, can be a Christian position and from precisely the same motives and principles as used above. The key difference is the analytical assessment of the Establishment for patience—"Rome wasn't built in a the past performance of "liberal plans and people" it is fairly easy to conclude that the present system won't work. Appeals of the Establishment for patience—"Rome wasn't built in a day"; "Look at the progress we've made so far"—make little sense to the poor and the disinherited. To say "The Irish made it; why can't you?" is to betray both one's racism and one's lack of understanding. Further, as our country and its institutions get bigger and more powerful, people—especially the poor and the black—become even more powerless.

Finally, while Christian ethics has always provided certain grounds for revolt and overthrow of tyranny, and while we do not have a tyrant in America now, it can be argued that we do have a kind of organizational, bureaucratic, technical tyranny which is almost as repressive. There is no one "bad guy." There are vast structures of "process," "systems," "procedures," and "orders of control" that are impersonal, vague, powerful, and apparently immune to both reform and change. It is this technological climate which young people refer to as "dehumanizing." This is the kind of tyranny which many believe must be abolished. Whether the change of the system is to be brought about by violent revolution, gradual evolution, or by alternate shocks of "confrontation violence" and "cool use of power"—"any means"—is another set of problems. My point is this: it is a valid Christian position to conclude that our present system needs to be replaced.

If abolishment of our present system is the conclusion we come to, then we will also need to point out the vague and pervasive difficulties that are inherent in this choice. Effective change of a whole system without some kind of revolution is unlikely. And if a revolution does occur, the dangers of either anarchy or a new tyranny worse than the old one are very great. There have not been many American colonial revolutions in history. And there is no guarantee that we could be successful in trying one again, especially since it would be against ourselves. The proposals that are drawn up to replace our present mixed capitalist-socialist model are exceedingly vague, ideal, and obscure. They strain one's credulity about man's virtue in general, and even more one's faith in the reformers.

So where does this lead us? I believe in "reform within the system," but I think that I understand and respect those who go for "abolishing the system." But what we all need within the household of faith is to acknowledge our faults and make clear our precarious moral mixes. We should *not*, I would insist, try to prove that our respective ethical choices are morally justifiable. Moral justification is the attempt to prove that our actions are right and that we are more right than wrong in what we are doing. All the emphasis is spent on highlighting the "right," emphasizing our noble goals and high motives. It is this kind of endeavor which tends to blur the weaknesses, simplify the ambiguities, and cover over the evils. It is not long before we polarize positions, throw labels at each other, and end up in idolatrous absolutizing.

I am trying to argue that the chief value of a Christian ethical system is *not* to justify but to define and describe the moral mixes in situations. Therefore the emphasis is to highlight the nature of the complexities, to emphasize the relative evils as well as the relative goods, and to discern the available options, the realistic choices. Let us look at a "specific" example: the highly controversial busing problem that surfaced in the spring of 1972. A Richmond, Virginia, federal judge ruled that children in the inner-city schools must be bused out to the suburban schools. The basic reason for the decision was the familiar situation in which the inferior quality schools were those in the city; the higher quality schools were those in suburbia. As might also be surmised, the inner-city schools were mostly black, the suburban mostly white. The issue soon became a national one. I shall not debate the pros and cons, but I do wish to emphasize two points. First, the problem became so controversial and emotional that one could not fairly categorize people on either side. The political and racial spectrum was demonstrated on all sides. Other issues were soon added, slogans and clichés appeared: "No forced racial balance," "Unconstitutional," "Un-American," "Reactionary," and the like. Everyone sought to justify his position, not as partly right but as totally right. Yet to any trained observer, it was obvious from the start that the original busing bill and the court order to have it implemented were both imperfect, limited, mixed policies. Legitimate defense and criticism and opposition were needed. Instead, people rushed to assert either/or—total right vs. total wrong. Defenders were forced to make ridiculous claims for the virtues and good effects of busing on education. Opponents conjured up evils and disasters that would never occur. What was needed was incisive ethical and practical analysis; what occurred was fearful fantasizing and self-justification.

The second point that I wish to stress is that in the busing controversy, the pressure for moral purity led to the easy conscience and to the neglect of the problem. The basic issue of inferior education for city children, most of whom are black, of course remains unmet. It seems to me that if we believe a specific policy or bill is inadequate or wrong, we have an equal responsibility at that very time to replace the measure with something better. In the Richmond case, the *least* the opponents could have done was to suggest that the money to be saved by no busing be put into upgrading the ghetto schools, or some other alternative. As it was, everybody was let off the moral hook; only the children in the ghetto continued to be neglected.

If one combines these two points, then the conclusion is, it seems to me, to emphasize again the need to return the use of ethics to the business of clarification rather than to moral justification.

Domestic Politics

One last brief test of the use of our Christian ethics approach is in the area of domestic politics. Here again it should be noted that the pietistic tradition in Christianity stands strongly against relating the gospel to political issues. In response, I must firmly state my strong disagreement with pietistic ethics. Failure to apply Christian ethics to political problems does not result in a neutral position as pietists often think. More often, the failure to relate the gospel in this area results in actual support of the *status quo*. Thus, Billy Graham's reference to the Vietnam war as "purely political" meant that he chose, willingly or not, to ignore the murderous Viet Cong assassination of village chiefs and our barbarous "carpet bombing" of Hanoi. His silence also resulted in the support of the war policies of both administrations, Democratic and Republican.

Similarly, in domestic issues, the pietist tends to be a political atheist. That is, domestic politics is politics and therefore presumably it is neither a religious nor a moral domain. But pietists vote and act in politics. If their political activity is not informed by Christianity, it must be guided by some other set of values. They are the various cultural values of liberals, conservatives, "middle Americans," "hard-hats," youth, labor, and management. The point is that such values and actions are not criticized nor informed by our Christian faith. Hence most of us are political and economic atheists.

It should also be fairly obvious that in my description and criticism of pietism that this critique applies to most of us Christians. While pietism is an identifiable tradition, nevertheless it has influenced the majority of us—more than we would like to confess, and perhaps more than we know. Therefore, it seems essential that we acknowledge the influence, get it out in the open, and account for it. Earlier in this chapter, we have noted the positive contributions of pietism, but, because of its great dangers and its opposition to our whole understanding of Christian ethics, we must be blunt in calling attention to the lack of pietistic Christian social ethics, and in charging pietists with political atheism.

Now, however, we must see how it is impossible to use Christian ethics in political issues without falling into the dangers that pietists proclaim. So again, as in all of my previous examples I begin with Christian love. I have said that this kind of love means caring about people and caring about what happens to them. If people are misgoverned, disenfranchised, denied equal justice before the law, these are political problems, but they are also moral issues. If we care about people and morality, then we have a responsibility to do something or to see that something is done to help.

Next, if we draw upon our natural law tradition and other noble principles, we have learned that a state is necessary, that politics is the way in which a state is governed, and that the two basic purposes of a state (and therefore of politics) are to prevent chaos and injustice, and to "promote the general welfare and secure the blessings of liberty to ourselves and our posterity" (from the preamble to the Constitution!).

Thus far, then, caring love and natural and constitutional principles lead us to be concerned and to seek action in political issues. The next steps obviously land us in the vast area of "situations," i.e., political parties, policies, and persons. Since I have noted earlier that assessments of any moral "situation" can vary, it follows that no one can claim that his evaluation is the only Christian one. Likewise because of our theological view of the nature of man, society, and history, only an idiot could assert that his political party is *the* Christian one and the opposing party the devilish one. There is nothing in the best of the Protestant and Catholic traditions which permits a Christian to equate a political party with either the saints or the Kingdom of God. The idolatrous blasphemy of the medieval Crusades should be the reminder of our earlier sins.

Other fallacious reasons for supporting either of our major political parties should be noted. For example, whether one likes or dislikes the personality of the President is irrelevant, if it remains on the level of "like" only. To illustrate from personal experience: a familiar slogan in the 1950's was "I Like Ike." To this I would often reply, "I *love* my wife, but I wouldn't vote for her for President." The rise of what some observers have labeled as the "personality cult" underlines our point. Of course, the personality of a President is important on the level of whether he is a stable, sane, responsible, and capable person. But whether we individuals like or dislike his public characteristics is irrelevant. Or to sharpen the point by another type of illustration, one can ask, "Would you rather be operated on by a gruff, taciturn, and highly competent surgeon, or by a nice, friendly, incompetent surgeon?" In short, competency is a better criterion than pleasantness.

Another difficulty in assessing the political parties and their people and policies is the use of rhetoric and slogans. The discerning Christian should know by now that while a certain amount of rhetoric is inevitable, he should not be taken in by slogans and clichés. Our understanding of the sin of man and the complexities of problems should save us from being beguiled by simplistic answers. But somehow most of us do not seem able to resist such easy "outs," and so we go along and vote just as everyone else does. Insofar as we do this, we only underline our need to draw upon the resources of our Christian faith. When we turn again to our ethical resources, we will find that Christian love and ethical principles provide guidance. For example, let us now apply our Christian ethics and its process to our political parties. The primary criterion for evaluating any political party is social justice. This means we will ask the following yardstick question: Which party, overall, tends to deal most effectively with the tough human injustice situations such as the ghetto poor, the rural poor, tax inequities, abuse of privileged power, economic exploitation, unfair taxes, and government interference with legitimate businesses?

While both parties make slogan overtures to many of these basic human problems, there are discernible differences between the parties over the years. At times, the Democrats have done a great deal toward trying to meet some of the problems of the poor. At other times, they have ignored and even fostered cruel racism. Similarly, the Republicans have sometimes tried to curb irresponsible unions and wild spending, but at other times they have obviously catered to the wealthy at the expense of the poor. And both parties stand indicted for their playing upon our anticommunist fears, increasing the power and secrecy of the Presidency, and dragging their feet on serious reforms to relieve racism and poverty. Nevertheless, at any given election time, it is possible, with effort, to discern significant differences between the parties and their policies.

Note that I have *not* described one man and one issue as the determining criterion for support in an election. While the Presidential candidate is or will be the leader and for that reason heavily influential, nevertheless the personnel he attracts and the overall values of the party are equally important. A one-issue vote is a simplistic answer that ignores the vast array of complex problems and programs. Also, our Christian theology informs us that the idea that "one good man can reform the system" is extremely limited. Precisely because most institutions are so large, they tend to overwhelm the few "good men" within them. We shall deal with this issue in the next chapter. But the problem is relevant in the political area. Often it is only by the use of political power that many "systems," institutions, and processes can be reformed. For example, one good man in the Department of Agriculture is not able to reform the farm subsidies program, but Congressional pressure or appropriations can effectively change such policies. To effect changes one must support political powers and parties; one vote for one man on one issue is relatively ineffectual. Thus our Christian ethics urge us actively to support and critically to vote for groups and political parties, not in blind allegiance, but in vigorous and careful independent action.

Lastly, our Christian ethics remind us that a major work of love is reconciliation. With regard to politics, reconciliation means that our ultimate goal is an understanding, diverse community. The sentimental word has been brotherhood; a more profound word would be "humanhood." This word intends to recognize and connote the facts of human diversity, the mixture of good and evil in all of us, but it also recognizes our essential identity as a people, as a nation, and as a vast, diverse community. After a contest or a conflict, we cannot long endure if daily life becomes only an angry truce while we gird up for the next contest. If we are to survive as a democracy, some attempts to reconcile opposing peoples and parties are essential. I must stress again that reconciliation does *not* mean political or ideological agreement. It does mean respect for each others' values and convictions. It also means some degree of common agreement on the preciousness of democracy, the need for tolerance, the acknowledgment of one's own weaknesses, and, finally, the desire to get along with each other. We do not have to "like" everybody else; what matters is that *we* see all people as human beings of worth and individuality, as children of God, regardless of what they think or how they vote. This is the hard part of the gospel. As any person active in politics knows, it is very difficult to regard one's political opponent as "a child of God." Other phrases come more quickly to mind! Yet precisely because it *is* so difficult to seek reconciliation, so hard to maintain democracy in the face of diversity and conflict, we need to draw strength from the resources of our faith.

I could say many more things about the relationship of Christian ethics to domestic politics. In fact, a whole book or even two could scarcely cover all the problems that need clarification in such a relationship. The following pages, though brief, will set forth ways in which Christian ethics could be used in the area of politics. Even so, I cannot conclude this section without a brief discussion of the problem of compromise in ethics and morals.

For most people the very word "compromise" has a bad connotation. One often hears the phrase "He compromised his morals." What is usually meant by this charge is that a person abandoned his moral ideals for a lower set of values. The meaning seems to emphasize a giving up of morality. Thus, a person may assert that he believes in the Sermon on the Mount as a sufficient moral guide. But when confronted by a hard-nosed business competitor or a threat from the Russians, he cannot practice this "love-your-enemies stuff." When a person retaliates against such an enemy, he is usually charged with compromising his beliefs, meaning, in effect that the Sermon on the Mount is "noble and true, but not in this situation. A fellow has to eat to survive, you know." So we say he has abandoned the Sermon, he has compromised his ethic.

There is, however, another meaning to the word "compromise." This other connotation denotes the act of choosing between imperfect alternatives. It does not mean abandoning an ideal. It does mean a recognition that one is achieving less than the ideal. The radical difference is that here one uses the ethical principle or moral ideal as a yardstick to choose between several alternatives. One is not giving up the ideal; he is, instead, using it to make a moral choice. The word "compromise" is here used to denote with rigorous honesty that the alternatives are indeed less than ideal.

To strengthen this point, note the contrast in meanings of the same word: in popular usage, "compromise" means that one has an ideal, is faced with an unideal choice and, for a variety of reasons, abandons the ideal, chooses the "real" and then tries to justify it on other, lesser, moral grounds such as "enlightened self-interest" or patriotism. In Christian usage, "compromise" means that one very consciously uses some ideal like love in order to find which alternative comes near-est to "the loving thing to do." Christian realism makes us aware that our choice is indeed unideal, but it is the "best available" or "the lesser of two evils." Thus, we have not aban-doned love; we have applied it. Compromise, therefore, is the integrity that reminds us of the imperfections in life, and in ourselves. But compromise is not the abandonment of our ethic; it is precisely the use of it.

It may well be that because the popular meaning of the term is so broad, it is not helpful for us to use the word "com-promise" anymore. Perhaps we had better use some other word such as "application," or "ethical approach," or "realistic assessment." In any case, it is of some importance that we at least do not use the word incorrectly or convey the wrong meaning. What matters is that we understand how Christian ethics can be made relevant to realistic problems.

Conclusions

Let us now review the essence and structure of the synthesis of the ethical traditions that we have employed. In the ex-amples described in the areas of personal and social ethics I have deliberately chosen the most complicated, controversial, and emotional problems. My hope here has been that if I could demonstrate that Christian ethics can offer some help, guid-ance, and direction to moral action on the most difficult moral issues, it would also be useful in the smaller and less vexing problems. Doubtless, some may feel that my "answers" to the "big issues" are something less than incisive and world-shaking. But my primary concern has not been to find "the answer" to: sex, war, peace, or racism. My chief aim has been to describe the structure and content by means of which a Christian can make moral distinctions resulting in effective action. My argu-ment is not that there exists a unique revelation from God on a specific issue; but my hope is that the processes and meth-ods which we have used make for sharper understanding, more profound application, and therefore more effective moral action.

So let us review the structure and its content. First, I started with "our one and only absolute"—Christian love. After its careful definition, I proceeded to indicate its many uses. That is to say, love is a motive, a power, and an attitude; but its characteristics also provide us with certain values and goals: reconciliation, hunger to do justice, the search for peace, help and care for persons, and many others. Ethically, Christian love is the motivating power, the end goal or ideal, but it is also the continuing ambience, attitude, or "style" of moral living. Love, then, is our top criterion, our greatest power. It is our ethical Ultimate.

Secondly, human reason must be used to its fullest capacity. It is a necessary tool in applying love to specific problems. Reason can help us obtain knowledge about the "situation," analyze options, sort out conflicting values and principles, balance competing needs.

Thirdly, from reason and natural law we also obtain many necessary principles, ideals, and goals: justice, freedom, equality, brotherhood, prudence, peace, fortitude, individuality, and our much-talked-of rights to "life, liberty, and the pursuit of happiness."

Fourthly, since our theology informs us about the nature of sin, the limits of reason, and the misuse of principles, as well as the complexities and ambiguities of "facts" and situations, we are aware that the application of love and principles is neither simple nor easy. Therefore flexibility in application is essential.

Fifthly, we know that the nature of problems and situations greatly determine both the application of ethical principles and the alternatives available. This is another way of saying that we must emphasize "the need to know the situation." This also assumes that one must draw upon secular knowledge from any and all sources in order to more fully understand situations.

Finally, I have emphasized that the primary way in which this process should be used is not to establish moral justification, but to achieve moral clarification. If there is anything new in our proposed synthesis between the ethical traditions of Rome and Geneva, it is only the affirmation that the primary purpose of Christian ethics and morals is clarification, description, and action. The problem of whether a Christian action is justified, righteous, morally valid, or ethically superior to a previous condition, *is* the province of worship, theology, and faith. So we say it again: *The* purpose of Christian ethics and morals is, simply, to "tell it like it is" and then to "feed my sheep."

This is the heart of our proposal for a synthesis between natural law and the ethics of love. The rest of our suggestions are debatable and adjustable ways of using the structure and its ingredients. Before we conclude our discussion of the synthesis or announce a "Hegelian" alliance, we think it advisable to devote a chapter to some problems that remain.

Chapter
VII

SOME REMAINING PROBLEMS

Two huge, relatively new, unsolved and urgent problems that must be dealt with are technology and social systems.

First, in using the term "technology," I do not mean it in the narrow sense of new machines or big tools. Most labor-saving devices, giant road-building machines and huge communications networks by themselves are not serious problems to man. In spite of occasional breakdowns and some misuse, it can be argued, I think, that their benefits to man in terms of efficient service and relief from drudgery far outweigh any minor disadvantages.[25]

Technology, in the larger sense of the word, means systems in which machines play a large part of the planning and purposes of a process or institution. This brings to the fore the problems created by computers and cybernetic systems which are often the heart of every large production. Computers are fantastically fast and efficient. When used for relatively small and specific technical problems, they are enormously helpful. But when used for wider social problems, or for problems that have social impact, then ethical issues appear. Psychological models and political predictions can be projected. Economic forecasts are often derived from computerized data. Foreign policy can be influenced by projections of "enemy capability" in nuclear weaponry. While one obvious ethical area is the use of computer data, another perhaps more serious and less obvious issue is the problem of the programmer. Who and what values are operative in the operators? Is the computer properly programmed to include human variables and values?

If we do not raise these types of questions, then computers will give out not only partial but also false information. In nuclear "war games" theories, for instance, as noted earlier, one common factor has been the assumption that America could take twenty million casualties without having to surrender or to die economically. Much above that level, the computer formulas assume disaster. My query is: Who programmed the machine that spewed out the statement that we could survive twenty million deaths? How do "they" know that we would, or would want to? One can raise all kinds of similar value questions, all of them highly debatable. Yet it is obvious that a computer cannot settle the rightness or wrongness of any of the basic value issues. So our point is not that computers are evil; they are not. It is the system of programming, the purposes of the use of analysis—that needs careful ethical attention.

Similarly, in cybernation, the self-regulating machines of tomorrow are enormously efficient and helpful. Their ethical threat is not that they are machines. It is that they are part of a system that is designed and maintained by a few persons but has power over many. Here, too, we have not only the ethical problem of values but also the matter of power. What checks are there or ought there to be on the cybernetic planners and the system itself? There is little doubt that large cybernetic systems will create massive unemployment at worst, and much leisure for most people at best. This will create the problem of whether we have a culture adequate to handle a life of leisure. Our present "work ethic" is clearly unsuited for such a task. Should such problems be included in cybernetic planning? [26] Are there sufficient feedback processes to include enough human variables? Many proposed economic cybernetic models are very thorough in including people's economic necessities, but they are often lacking in people's economic desires. That is to say, obviously man needs food, but does he need an art studio or music room or carpentry shop? He doesn't need those rooms in order to survive economically. But he still might want such a space in his apartment. It is clearly a cost item and therefore an economic problem not only for the architect and the builder, but also for the finance company. So here we have a question not just of economic need, but also of economic desire. And that, of course, spills over into psychological and aesthetic needs and desires. Are we sure that the system takes all of these factors into account?

One can readily see how the problems will increase when cybernetic systems are enlarged to deal with urban housing and planning, with city communications and power systems. Strict needs can be met efficiently by these machines. But the ethical and moral issues appear when we raise the questions about other needs and human wants and desires. These types of "needs" may or may not be as essential as survival needs. But in any case, they ought to be considered, analyzed, and evaluated. Such a system certainly needs plenty of variables planned into its feedback process! Meanwhile, there must be a plan for a permanent system of checks and balances on the policymakers, the programmers, and the interpreters.

Another area of moral concern in the computer field is the data banks. These systems are marvels of efficiency, but the possible misuse of them can be enormously damaging. One mistake in one symbol can ruin a man's credit rating. Raw data, isolated from the total picture, can be used to destroy a person's reputation. Thus business data banks can harm one's economic life. Government data banks can ruin one's vocational life. The U.S. Army's secret surveillance of political candidates plus that of some congressmen and senators, and even of one Supreme Court Justice (Thurgood Marshall) is a shocking example of misuse. Clearly, then, the public needs strong protection against those who collect, select, and interpret the "profiles."

In this short book it is impossible to treat adequately the deeper dimensions of these problems. But I believe it is humanly and ethically necessary to call attention to these relatively new and pervasive issues. The shortest summary of this brief description might be: it isn't the machine that dehumanizes, it is the system that tends to enslave man. Thus, the systems of many modern machines constitute a major part of large economic and political structures. This fact then leads into the larger area of social systems and whether such giant structures create equally enormous ethical and moral problems.

In the previous chapter, I noted that some of the basic issues in war and racism raise the old problem of "reform from within" or "change of the whole system." We are forced to return to this same issue when we are confronted by the huge system of our contemporary life. On almost any level and with any basic problem today one is met with the structure of a large process. If one is calling for economic reform, one is faced by vast and powerful industrial representation and power. If one works for political reform, the two giant parties, plus traditional ways of doing things in Congress, easily stifle change. There is little doubt that the majority of persons feel totally helpless to effect any change in the areas of economics and politics. Faced with such giants of power, it is little wonder. Yet it is the feeling of helplessness which leads to the conviction of many people that it is impossible to reform within. If it seems even more unlikely that the whole system could be abolished, that is probably true, but the desperation of such a revolutionary call is more understandable. If one wants a little more justice; if one has tried all the lawful and usual ways, and still all efforts have been ignored, then what can one do? It is in this type of situation that the youthful explosions over the invasion of Cambodia must be understood. It is important to recall that the majority voted for Lyndon Johnson in the Presidential election of 1964 largely because of his promise *not* to get us involved in Vietnam, since their other choice would have been Barry Goldwater with his bellicose stand. President Johnson's decision not to run again for office was greatly influenced by his decline in popularity just because of his failure to keep this promise. With his removal from the Presidential competition, it seems to many that, at last, public opinion *did matter* and that changes *could* be effected. Thus the election of Richard Nixon seemed to confirm this, especially since there is no doubt that a major part of his victory in 1968 was his oft-repeated claim that he had "a plan for peace."

Consequently, two years later when Nixon ordered the land invasion of Cambodia and the air invasion of Laos, many people, especially the young, felt betrayed. For had not the majority voted against Goldwater and for Johnson in the name of peace, and, instead, got war? In other words, the people rose up in protest and, with Johnson out of the race, voted for Nixon and his peace platform. But then came the Cambodian invasion and once more the people found themselves betrayed, this time by the Republican leaders. When the majority feel they are double-crossed by both leading political parties, what can they do? That is, roughly, the way it was in 1970. That the Cambodian outbursts were followed by at least two years of calm on the campus only confirms my point. It was not a healthy "peace." The lack of outbursts and violence were not due to new reforms. The calm was a product of cynicism, helplessness, and despair. The common college response was "What's the use? You just can't change anything." So most students turned inward to their own problems, became more hedonistic and, outwardly, decided to get their merit badges, to carve out a little niche in the system, and no longer to tangle with problems of reform, justice, racism, and "all that." This feeling of social impotence has spread, and most concerned people, young and old, today feel increasingly helpless to effect any reforms. This is one other major reason why the reform within vs. the abolition of the system has become a growing ethical dilemma.

Still another and more subtle but pervasive cause is the

style of life that has been developed by those who work in large bureaucratic organizations. Most bureaucracies are hierarchical in structure and also have some kind of rating or promotional or efficiency process. It is a built-in natural "system" which thereby forces one to please the boss or the evaluator. This automatically tends to induce supine agreement: "Yes, sir." While men at the top often call for men of initiative, daring, and innovation, it is a fact with the personnel downstairs and because of the structure of the system, few innovators or critics survive; the mousey yes-men do. Studies have shown that employment testing in some firms is clearly designed to weed out the nonconformist. Other businesses send around "cultural suggestions," e.g., that employees might find it advantageous if they joined a church, helped out in the Little League and charity drives. When President Nixon returned from China, some department heads at the Department of Health, Education, and Welfare were told to "urge" their employees to attend the arrival at 9 P.M. at Andrews Air Force Base. If one was trying for a promotion or higher job rating, it would be very difficult to refuse such an "urging."

Whether it is in business or in government or in the military, the bureaucratic structural system is essentially a stifling and conformist process. To be sure, there are some compensating features which enable many people to endure and perhaps receive some comfort. Since there are usually "standard operating procedures," rules and regulations, and customary ways of doing things, there is considerable security and reliability in one's job. Few difficult decisions are required, no precarious or daring innovations are needed. Therefore one is seldom "wrong" or responsible. One "goes by the book." Therefore if something does go wrong, it was "the system," not me. Anyone who has ever had to go to a bureaucrat with a complicated or unusual problem knows what usually happens. Because it is an out-of-the-ordinary problem, the bureaucrat does not want to handle the issue at all. Or if he is forced to do so, he will try to reduce the problem to a simple rule or practice. He will then probably say "No! it can't be done," or push it along to somebody else.

In short, within the system and its rules, there is a type of security and reliable routine with living wage and retirement benefits and some chance of promotion, *if* you play the game. But the price of all this is the subtle, constant, and pervasive pressures of conformity, blandness, narrowness, and passionless existence. The occasional *Reader's Digest* story of the daring, aggressive innovator who "hewed his way through a wall" of red tape to reach the top is true for the few. But vast millions remain enslaved to the hierarchical system, and it is essentially dehumanizing. These structures *do* curtail the human spirit, the forces of individuality and freedom. It is precisely this growing phenomenon that is largely responsible for many young people seeking a different life-style. It is also partly the reason for the increasing duality (if not schizophrenia) of those who are bureaucrats. Mouselike automatons by day or week, many try to become Lotharios or playboys by night, or James Bonds or golf heroes on the weekends. We are now faced with an increasing number of bureaucratic Walter Mittys.

Finally, this stifling bureaucratic culture is another significant reason for the contemporary feeling of helplessness in our social and vocational life. It contributes to the conclusion that one cannot really reform from within. Yet it also contributes to the desperation of cynicism, for when one looks at other political and social systems—for example, Sweden, Russia, and China—one can only see even more oppressive blandness (Sweden), more elaborate bureaucratic structures (Russia), and more rigid conformity (China). Little wonder that some groups have fled back to nature in rural communes! Our conclusion, then, appears to suggest that "reform from within" and "abolition of the whole system" *are both* unrealistic and impossible. This would seem to put an end to all social ethics, to all struggles for justice.

I do not fully concur with the above conclusion but do

acknowledge and agree that it is a persuasive and tenable estimate. If our present attitudes and practices and policies remain the same, the conclusion will probably be verified. However, I am a firm believer in the realistic possibility that effective changes can be made within the system and the system itself gradually (granted ups and downs) reformed. We cannot recite the history of all the changes that have been made so far, and any ethically sensitive person would agree that reforms have neither been fast nor widespread enough. Similarly, advances in the future will never satisfy our urgent demands nor the desires of the victims of injustice. So what is the evidence for the hope of ethical advance?

I see three major evidences and the first is that the Christian knows that there is no guarantee of moral success or automatic ethical progress. The cross is the reminder of the fact of tragedy in life and the fact that the good are often crucified. But the resurrection is also the reminder that defeat, evil, and death are not the final realities in life. This is God's world *and therefore* new possibilities for caring love will appear and new opportunities to seek new levels of justice will occur, often in situations where least expected. Who ever expected an elderly and unknown pope to shake up the Roman Church (John XXIII), or an ex-hustler and former drug addict, who had become a black Muslim, to give new dignity to blacks and to call for equal power and eventual racial reconciliation (Malcolm X)? The Christian continues to work for social justice not because he is assured of triumph or inevitable progress, but because love is what motivates him to act, and faith, and the hope that God may use his deeds.

The second ground for hope is my belief that the church is beginning, at last, to see that its individualistic approach to social problems is not enough. The pietistic tradition has operated on the assumption that private individuals within groups could effect reforms; but the church as an institution or as a group of Christians should not interfere in social issues. Their hope was that if they could convert the leader of a country, or the head of any business or social organization, or barring that, if they could plant a few morally influential Christians in the organization, the system would be reformed. With our vast modern structural powers, and the culture of bureaucracy that we have just described, it should be obvious that it is going to take more than the efforts of a few "good guys" to influence centers of power or to reform effectively a social structure. The present black power struggle understands this. The church is just beginning to see this point. But the cognizance is there and it will grow. It is also another reason why a synthesis or an alliance between the ethical traditions of Rome and Geneva could result in some much-needed ethical muscle.

My third reason for believing in the possibility of ethical advance and social reform is a somewhat paradoxical one. The two foremost perennial domestic moral scandals are poverty and racism. It is true that we always have the poor with us, and it is also true that the church, over the centuries, has done a pretty good job in ministering to and helping the poor through its continuing programs of food, clothing, and medical care. In fact, no other institution can match its record in this area. On the other hand, the church has not only been derelict in its social duty but has also contributed to economic and political systems that create or permit poverty. So there is an odd and unintentional historical irony of the church indirectly creating the conditions for poverty and then descending to care for its victims.

The church's record on racism has been far worse. The institution has not only contributed to racism, it has practiced racism itself, as well as failed to help the victims. Only in recent years have we begun to respond correctly to this vast injustice.

The nature of the paradoxical grounds for ethical hope in the areas of poverty and racism is this: these two problems are so vast, so deep, and so very evil that I find it very difficult to understand how the church—including Christian clergy and laity alike—could fail to see its complicity in the structures that cause poverty and racism. I have the same feelings about Congress: how could any reasonably ethical humanist continue perennially to favor the rich and the powerful, and regularly ignore the poor and the disinherited, and then compound the immorality by righteously voting for peripheral measures with insulting handouts and tokenism? Thus, I believe that if the church and the Congress (and therefore the citizens at large) continue to ignore these two crucial domestic ethical problems, both the church and the nation will be judged by the Lord of history. Since I cannot know the when or the how of such a judgment, I will not venture to predict specifics. I would not be surprised if the visible church became totally irrelevant to modern man, and at best became a small comfort station alongside the highway of life, into which a few elderly people would enter to seek some kind of refuge or consolation. That is one real possibility.

Moreover, because such a situation is becoming apparent, I believe that a creative minority of laity and clergy within Rome and Geneva will gather together, join forces, and seek as a group to "redeem the time, for the days are evil." I believe there is a real possibility that part of the visible church will be changed, that an ethical synthesis, if not a theological one, can be effected, and that a new visible form of the church will appear. Finally, I believe that this new church will find its way to act as a group, to obtain cultural power, and to use it effectively and responsibly. The source of this hope is not a dreamy, wistful idealism but the empirically observable hunger and desire of many Christian laymen inside and outside of the contemporary church. Though the clergy cannot control or direct it, happily, I believe the Holy Spirit will lead the way.

Chapter
VIII

THE FRUITS OF USING CHRISTIAN ETHICS

While one hopes that there would be many fruits growing out of this proposed alliance of Roman and Protestant ethics, I would expect at least two important ones to appear: a continuing ethical culture, and a new and better use of Christian ethics and moral theology. We shall deal first with the need for a continuing ethical culture. Part of this writer's professional research over the years has involved him in fairly extensive interviewing of decision makers in business and politics. Since the projects have always entailed finding out how people make moral and ethical decisions two by-products of my research have been the study of the influence of ethics on practical decisions, and the study of the transmission of moral values from a culture to its people. Obviously, one cannot open huge cans of peas labeled "How to Absorb Moral Values," or "How Ethics Can Best Be Taught," or "The Transvaluation of Values in Culture," digest the contents, and expect results!

Nevertheless, it will not surprise the experts in the field that during my research I discovered one very significant phenomenon. It is this: most people do *not* agonize or reflect over moral decisions. Indeed, most people do not even regard most decisions as moral problems; they tend to regard them as technical. For example, when asked "What are your chief

moral dilemmas as a politician?" most congressmen replied
that they had no moral dilemmas! When pressed to reply as to
how they resolved conflicts between personal integrity vs.
party loyalty, or the use of power against a political opponent,
they would preface their remarks with "Oh! but that's a political problem!" Their thinking was that a moral dilemma was
a temptation to violate the Ten Commandments. They thought
I was asking "Do you sleep with your secretary?" Since most
congressmen don't, they could truthfully say "No, we don't
have many moral dilemmas."

Similarly, in interviewing many business executives, they
too denied any moral dilemmas. They believed that ethics and
morals were limited to being nice to employees. Since most
contemporary firms are "nice" (fringe benefits, clean wash-
rooms, piped-in music, grievance committees, etc.), they could
rightly say that they had few moral dilemmas. But when asked
about the ethical dilemmas that might be involved in the
setting of prices, the production of luxury goods, quality control and advertising procedures, most businessmen would reply, "But those are purely economic problems."

Quite apart from the issue of whether various problems are
technical or moral, the common denominator among the majority of men interviewed was this: Even if there was a moral
dilemma present and recognized, most men asserted that they
made their moral decision pretty much spontaneously and in
accord with commonly accepted standards or morals. Very
few engaged in any deep reflection, ethical anguish, or moral
"sweat." This led me to the conclusion that the general culture
in which a person lives is probably the most influential factor
in determining his moral behavior. I am sure this is a truism
for many professional anthropologists, sociologists, and others.
I am sure there are also many other factors involved in the
making of moral decisions. My only point is to stress these
two significant issues: the influence of culture, and the way
culture is transmitted. Most people do not agonize over
moral decisions; they tend to make choices pretty much in

terms of their total upbringing, personality, and cultural orientation. The relating of one's theology to ethics, the careful rational analyzing of which ethical principles are applicable, and the understanding of the blend of good and bad in everyone as I have been emphasizing in this book is just not worked out by most people.

Therefore, *one* possible helpful use of our suggested ethical synthesis may be to contribute to a more permanent ethical tradition in a changing culture. That is to say, if there is a model, or a body of ethical principles, a spirit of flexibility, an ethos of caring love, there may be some chance of transmitting all this to the next generation. If there is a discernible corpus of ethical and natural law principles, and a life-style based upon them, it might survive a changing of both cultures and systems, or at least provide some standard above the flow and flux of change.

I have stated earlier that one of the weaknesses of Roman Catholic natural law ethics and moral theology was that, in its transmission down through history, its tendency has been to develop rigidity, legalism, and rigor mortis via overabundant rules. Meanwhile, the weakness of Protestant situational ethics has been that there was nothing to transmit except a vague love and an equally vague principle of flexibility. Neither tradition, by itself, therefore, can offer much to this empirical and cultural problem. By contrast, it is my hope that the proposed ethical synthesis can offer some contribution in the form of embodying and preserving a pervasive system of values under the ethos of a flexible love.

In addition to this value structure, new methods of teaching successive generations will have to be devised. As with secular educational methods, so with religious "instruction," there are in process much-needed intensive changes and experiments. However, I have the old feeling that whatever new ways of education may prove to be valid, the most effective method will be the overall behavior of Christians. Our present style of life is indistinguishable from secular styles; our ethical behavior is largely non-Christian. If our ethical synthesis results in some discernible life-style, it may enhance whatever new valid method is developed. To be sure, we shall always need our professional theologians and ethical experts. The difficult and complex theoretical problems will always need precise and intense study, analysis, and articulation, as is true of all major areas of human concern. Even so, theory and practice mutually fertilize each other. And the balance in the future will probably have to be weighted toward the development of new Christian life-styles, new ways of living.

This particular suggested model for a synthesis may not be adequate. Some may feel that it is not precise and clear enough. Others may feel that it is too dogmatic, too big and not simple or flexible enough. What matters is not *this* particular model. I offer it only as a sample with the hope that it will encourage others to build on it, or to discard it and produce other and better ones.

The second result of the ethical synthesis that I would like to see occur is a different use of the enterprises of moral theology and Christian ethics. In the previous chapter, I discussed some of the past dangers involved when the church and/or individuals use ethics to justify one's righteous moral behavior. Accordingly, I now wish to emphasize what I think is a more effective and proper role.

Moral theology should be used to relate theological insights and doctrines to ethical principles and to moral actions. Thus, in the discussion of nuclear morality, the need for and the relevance of a Christian interpretation of history were stressed. Moral theology, it seems to me, is precisely the vehicle for analyzing the problem and relating theological insights to moral choices. Moral theology *should not* be used to justify the person or the institution. It should be used to help relate theology to action and to define the issues involved in situations.

Similarly, Christian ethics should be used to convey values and principles and then to apply them to moral situations.

Ethics should *not* be used to prove that any given action was righteous or unrighteous. Simplistic "either/or" labels should be rejected in advance. The chief purpose of applied Christian ethics should be to analyze the morality of various situations, e.g., what are the moral and immoral mixes involved? what are the ambiguities? what is the rough percentage of justice over injustice? In short, we are saying: Let us divorce ethics from the problem of personal or institutional righteousness.

This would help reduce some of the moral "mix." For so long as part of my motive is to make sure that I am at least partly righteous then this will surely color some of my moral analysis. By contrast, if I regard ethics as an analytical tool designed to fashion the true picture of the moral problem at hand, I may get a more accurate view of the situation. I may also be able to see more clearly the moral mix of relative good and evil both in myself and in the external issue. If I am not worried about my status, I may be able to see more clearly the real nature of the moral situation.

So let us enthrone moral theology as the medium for relating theology to ethics to morals, and let ethics be the container of values and principles as well as the chief tool of application and analysis: the ethical "telling it like it is."

Meanwhile, what shall be done with liturgy and worship? Ethically speaking, I would argue that the two chief purposes of liturgy and worship are first moral, the forgiveness of the doer; and secondly ethical, the renewal of the person. Forgiveness is essential in the moral life because, as we all know, our choices are mixtures of relative good and evil, and our motives are usually combinations of egoism and love. Of course, one is not always responsible for the external evils. There is no need to agonize in guilt over the evils one is faced with in life. Yet when we do make choices and initiate courses of action, we are, in part, responsible for what we do. And we have been protesting strongly against the practice that lets us off completely from any accountability. Our proposed model tries to strike a balance between excessive guilt and excessive righteousness. Forgiveness by means of justification by faith is the recognition of the mixtures of good and evil inside and outside of us, and the awareness that we are accepted as full human beings precisely because we acknowledge the mixture and seek to love the more.

In seeking to love the more, we are faced with the need for renewal. Any honest person who has any degree of self-knowledge knows that he does not have the power to love as he ought to love. In terms of everyday moral action, any sensitive person also knows he does not do enough, care enough, forgive others enough, "go the second mile." The "old man" of egoism, and our own interests, problems, and concerns are always with us and often close out other persons' needs. And the smarter one is, the more plausible excuses one can give as to why he "cannot help at this time." Our Christian doctrine of man confirms what we know empirically, namely, that we do not love as we *ought* to love. Therefore, renewal through sanctification by the Holy Spirit is a continuing need.

In summary, then, the ancient argument about whether one can have ethics without religion (and vice versa) seems to me to be easily settled by any empirical test. To be sure, if one's highest ethical principle is to reach the nearest lamppost, one could achieve that without much help. But if one adopts the Christian faith, he knows right from the start that he cannot be "perfect, even as your Father which is in heaven." One soon learns, once he engages in moral actions and faces ethical dilemmas, that one neither knows enough nor is good enough to "go it alone." We need not only forgiveness and renewal, we need all the resources of our faith.

Liturgy and worship are among the chief ways by which a person can receive new power to love. The types and forms of worship may vary and change, but the essential need and Presence is there. As with some moral rules, if some ritual practices get in the way of experiencing God's love, they should be abandoned. Not all particular churches are necessarily households of faith. St. Swithins-in-the-Swamp may be more of a social club or cultural home than a place where the living God can be found. But again, as with rules, so with liturgy and worship, the fact that there is misuse is no reason to discard all rules or all rites or all churches.

In any event, it seems clear that in order to achieve ethical and moral power, we need to draw upon the resources of our religious faith. It is thus my conviction that if we understand the proper roles of—and the relation between—theology, ethics, morals, worship, and the church, our ethics will be truer and less self-righteous, and our moral actions will be more forthright and daring and effective.

The day of the private, lonely Christian trying to do good on his own within the vast social organizations of our time has passed. We need to band together, pool our resources and efforts and thereby provide some kind of moral power to influence "the principalities and powers" of the world. Finally, it is to be hoped that if this suggested model or synthesis is not the right one, other writers will come forward and propose more adequate ones. An ethical union between Rome and Geneva would surely increase the Christian witness and provide the Lord with a stronger instrument for his power.

NOTES

1. For a more complete listing of books with a brief comment on each, see the Bibliography.

2. Bernard Häring, *Toward a Christian Moral Theology*, p. 208.

3. James M. Gustafson, *Christ and the Moral Life*.

4. Robert C. Mortimer, *The Elements of Moral Theology*.

5. Outka and Ramsey (eds.), *Norm and Context in Christian Ethics*, pp. 92, 98.

6. Joseph Fletcher, *Situation Ethics: The New Morality* (title of chapter 8).

7. Paul Ramsey, *Deeds and Rules in Christian Ethics*.

8. Gustafson, *op. cit.*

9. H. Richard Niebuhr, *Christ and Culture*.

10. For an interesting example of Roman Catholic rethinking of some issues pertaining to the magisterium and infallibility, see Charles Curran (ed.), *Absolutes in Moral Theology* (Corpus Books, 1968). Daniel Maguire, in his chapter on "Moral Absolutes and the Magisterium," writes: "A dialogical magisterium does not claim infallibility of either Pope or bishop or laity; but *all* parts of the church are, together, the magisterium. It is not absolutely infallible, but it is the magisterium." (Pp. 105–106.)

11. A good summary of divine and natural law is given in Thomas A. Wassmer, *Christian Ethics Today*. See especially p. 86, where he quotes from an article by George M. Regan.

12. Carl Schurz (1859).

13. John Macquarrie, *Three Issues in Ethics*, p. 89.

14. This statement was made to the author in 1970 by a bishop of the Episcopal Church.

15. Deane W. Ferm, *Responsible Sexuality—Now* (The Seabury Press, 1971), p. 207.

16. *The Washington Post*, Feb. 7, 1972.

17. Some fine modern and contemporary examples of "Theology for Social Ethics" would include William Temple, *Nature, Man and God* (The Macmillan Company, 1934); Paul L. Lehmann, *Ethics in a Christian Context;* James Sellers, *Theological Ethics;* and Josef Fuchs, *Natural Law: A Theological Investigation.*

18. Paul Ramsey, *War and the Christian Conscience: How Shall Modern War Be Conducted Justly?* (Duke University Press, 1961).

19. *Ibid.*, p. 11.

20. Ramsey, *War and the Christian Conscience.*

21. For another way of thinking about war and ethical issues, I would recommend: Ralph B. Potter, *War and Moral Discourse.* This is, in my judgment, the most concise and beautifully clear presentation available. There is a long and excellent bibliography, which comprises almost half of this small paperback.

22. Ralph Potter has an excellent paragraph on this point (*op. cit.*, p. 61).

23. In some black plays and dramas and in some of the more sophisticated writings of Eldridge Cleaver and LeRoi Jones (Imamu Amiri Baraka), one can find manhood and freedom partly defined as "getting us a honkey" or "taking some with us next time." Some of this was a conscious attempt to parody "redneck culture," which often spoke of "getting us a nigger" or of sexual conquests of black women.

24. J. Deotis Roberts, *Liberation and Reconciliation: A Black Theology* (The Westminster Press, 1971); and James H. Cone, *A Black Theology of Liberation* (J. B. Lippincott Company, 1970).

25. A solid reply to many nobly intended but superficial articles against "dehumanization" is to be found in Denys L. Munby's book *God and the Rich Society* (Oxford University Press, 1961), especially chapters 6 and 7.

26. For a rousing and passionate concern for the need of creating a "cybernetic culture," see the writings of Alice Mary Hilton and those of Robert Theobald.

BIBLIOGRAPHY

This bibliography is not intended to be a complete list on the subjects covered in this book. A selection has been made, on a rather subjective basis, of books that I regard as significant, representative, or relevant at the present time.

Beach, Waldo, and Niebuhr, H. Richard (eds.), *Christian Ethics—Sources of the Living Tradition*, rev. ed. The Ronald Press Company, 1973. A concise historical survey with excellent examples and quotes from the major figures in ethics.

Bennett, John C., *Christian Ethics and Social Policy*. Charles Scribner's Sons, 1946. An early example of a modern "middle axiom" approach to social ethics.

Bonhoeffer, Dietrich, *Ethics*, ed. by Eberhard Bethge, tr. by Neville Horton Smith. London: SCM Press, Ltd., 1955. *The* provocative Christian "existential" book on ethics.

Brunner, Emil, *The Divine Imperative*, tr. by Olive Wyon. The Westminster Press, 1947. One of the great scholarly theological-ethical classics in the Protestant tradition.

Cave, Sydney, *The Christian Way*. Philosophical Library Press, 1951. A good basic Biblical summary with sample applications.

Dailey, Robert, *Introduction to Moral Theology*. Bruce Publishing Company, 1970. An easy-to-read presentation of a Roman Catholic natural law ethics.

Dodd, C. H., *Gospel and Law*. Cambridge University Press, 1950. The venerable New Testament scholar's Bampton Lectures spelling out the relation between gospel and law in the early New Testament period.

Fletcher, Joseph, *Moral Responsibility: Situation Ethics at Work*.

The Westminster Press, 1967. Further elaborates situation ethics and replies to critics.

——— *Situation Ethics: The New Morality.* The Westminster Press, 1966. The original best-selling statement of Protestant situational ethics.

Frankena, William K., *Ethics.* Prentice-Hall, Inc., 1963. A hard-headed and critical presentation of the various kinds of normative ethics. Refreshingly realistic!

Fuchs, Josef, *Natural Law: A Theological Investigation,* tr. by Helmut Reckter and John A. Dowling. Sheed & Ward, Inc., 1965. A standard sample of Roman Catholic natural law theory.

Gustafson, James M., *Christ and the Moral Life.* Harper & Row, Publishers, Inc., 1968. An excellent analysis of how various views of the nature of Christ lead to differing emphases in ethics.

Häring, Bernard, *Toward a Christian Moral Theology.* University of Notre Dame Press, 1966. A modern sample of a critical Roman Catholic natural law approach.

Kirk, Kenneth E., *Some Principles of Moral Theology.* Reprint of 1st ed., 1920. Longmans, Green & Co., Inc., 1957. An excellent liberal Anglican exposition of a natural law ethic.

Lehmann, Paul L., *Ethics in a Christian Context.* Harper & Row, Publishers, Inc., 1963. A scholarly and weighty presentation of Christian ethics in modern terms and categories of thought.

Macquarrie, John, *Three Issues in Ethics.* Harper & Row, Publishers, Inc., 1970. A succinct and brilliant analysis of three major problems in ethics today.

Mortimer, Robert C., *The Elements of Moral Theology.* London: A. & C. Black, Ltd., 1947. A clear exposition of moral theology by a conservative Anglican.

Niebuhr, H. Richard, *Christ and Culture.* Harper & Brothers, 1951. A seminal work analyzing the ethical effects of relating Christ to culture in various ways.

Niebuhr, Reinhold, *An Interpretation of Christian Ethics.* Harper & Brothers, 1935. The classic presentation of the "impossible possibility" ethics.

Outka, Gene H., and Ramsey, Paul (eds.), *Norm and Context in Christian Ethics.* Charles Scribner's Sons, 1968. Essays relating natural law to the Protestant love ethic tradition.

Potter, Ralph B., *War and Moral Discourse.* John Knox Press, 1969. A short, lucid account of the basic issues involved in Christian pacifism and nonpacifism, with a superb bibliography.

Ramsey, Paul, *Deeds and Rules in Christian Ethics,* enlarged ed.

Charles Scribner's Sons, 1967. A first-class presentation of a kind of Protestant natural law ethic.

———— *War and the Christian Conscience: How Shall Modern War Be Conducted Justly?* Duke University Press, 1961. One of the best books dealing with the subject of its title.

Sellers, James, *Theological Ethics*. The Macmillan Company, 1966. A good presentation of some central theological issues basic to any good ethics.

Waddams, Herbert, *A New Introduction to Moral Theology*. The Seabury Press, 1965. An excellent and concise critical presentation of a Christian natural law ethic.

Wassmer, Thomas A., *Christian Ethics Today*. Bruce Publishing Co., 1969. A good example of a liberal Roman Catholic discussion of the natural law ethic applied to some of today's issues.